Moses Hull

The contrast

Evangelicalism and Spiritualism Compared

Moses Hull

The contrast
Evangelicalism and Spiritualism Compared

ISBN/EAN: 9783337334789

Printed in Europe, USA, Canada, Australia, Japan

Cover: Foto ©Lupo / pixelio.de

More available books at **www.hansebooks.com**

THE CONTRAST:

EVANGELICALISM AND SPIRITUALISM

COMPARED.

By MOSES HULL,

AUTHOR OF "QUESTION SETTLED," "LETTERS TO ELDER MILES GRANT," "BOTH SIDES," "THAT TERRIBLE QUESTION," "THE SUPREMACY OF REASON," "THE WOLF IN SHEEP'S CLOTHING," ETC.

"For their rock is not as our Rock, even our enemies themselves being judges."
Deuteronomy xxxii. 31.

BOSTON:
WILLIAM WHITE AND COMPANY,
"BANNER OF LIGHT" OFFICE,
No. 14 HANOVER STREET.
1873.

PREFACE.

WHEN, in the preface to another volume about four years since, I promised this, I had no thought of keeping my friends in waiting so long. But this is a busy life, and especially a busy age; and other duties have pressed so continually, that, until now, I have not been able to answer this demand of my friends. Had it not been for acts of injustice on the part of "false brethren," I could not even now have found the time to have prepared this volume. One unrighteous act, that stripped me of the most of my earthly possessions, gave me time to write these pages.

Though the press gave me a severe castigation for once before stating that my thoughts were hastily thrown together, I must repeat the offence; the same is true of this volume. I have written this book in little snatches, on the cars and in boarding-houses, never having lost the opportunity for a single lecture, or an hour's work in consequence of it.

Newspaper scribblers need not tell me this is imperfect. I know it. Had I kept it from a hungry public until I could have found time to have revised and perfected it, I would have done them more injustice than I have in handing them this hastily prepared repast.

This book, too, has shaped itself; my plans have not been followed; matter I had prepared for it remains unpublished, while some that is here I had not intended should see the light for some time to come.

I have used the term Evangelicalism instead of Orthodoxy, when, individually, I should have preferred the latter. My reason is, the term Orthodoxy signifies one thing in the East, and another in the West; so that I could not make it so well serve my purpose.

Hoping this book may receive the favorable reception that has been accorded to my former works, I hand it out to a generous public,

Subscribing myself, as ever,

A Friend of Humanity,

MOSES HULL.

BOSTON, January 1, 1873.

CONTENTS.

CHAPTER I.

WHAT IS SPIRITUALISM?

PAGE

Author describes his own Spiritualism. — Division of the Subject. — Religion of Spiritualism. — Objections to the term Religion. — Ground of Objection. — First Ideas, God a Spirit. — Second, Man a Spiritual Being. — Is Man Infinite. — "Communion of Saints." — Revelation not infallible. — Some Parts of the Bible more important than others. — "Cause and Cure of Infidelity." — Burgon on the Bible. — What Spiritualism denies. — Total Depravity. — Who believes it. — Chicago Fire and its Lesson. — Atonement weighed in the Balance. — Man in the Garden. — Clark on Genesis ii. 16. — Benson on Same. — Buck and the Confession of Faith on the Penalty. — "Spiritual Death" defined. — Badly mixed. — Adam and Eve in Court. — A foolish Judge. — Adam's Dialogue with Men and Devils. — An unjust Judge. — The Principle applied to our Courts. — Conditions of vicarious Atonement. — Did Jesus die a spiritual Death? — How can Man be vicariously redeemed from Hell? — Formal Worship and our Duty. — Shall we ask the Blessing? — The Time for Worship and Sabbaths. — Vocal Prayer. — Jesus on public Prayer. — The Brotherhood of Man and its Corollaries. — Our Duty to the Family. — Endless Progression. — Man the Author of his own Heavens and Hells. — No Infallibility even among the Good. — Spiritual Philosophy and Philosophy of Spiritualism. — Source of Power. — Philosophy of Entrancement. — The inward Monitor. — No perfect Standard. — Science of making People good. — Rules of Life developed out of Conditions. — The Treatment of Sin. — Should Consumptives and Cripples be hung. — History of Spiritualism everywhere. — A. J. Davis's Prophecy. — Rapid Advancement of the Cause. — Foretold Evils have not followed. — The present Work. — Concluding Suggestions. 11

CHAPTER II.

COMPARATIVE EVIDENCE OF THE BIBLE AND SPIRITUALISM.

No necessary Antagonism. — Christian Arguments used for Spiritualism. — Nicodemus's Argument. — The Works of Jesus and Mediums compared. — Did Jesus raise the Dead? — Modern Resurrections. — Testimony of Daily Papers. — A man resuscitated after having been buried ten Months. — Mrs. Lancaster resurrected. — Resurrection of Rev. William Tennent. — Jesus did not always succeed. — The healing at Bethesda only one of a thousand. — Why did he not heal others? — The Pentecostal Evidences considered. — Same in Spiritualism. — Suicidal Argument against Spiritualism. — Silly Spiritualism and the Bible compared. — Jesus eating Fish and Spirits eating Apples. — "Devils and Darkness" of Bible Times. — Biblical Evidence not conclusive. — Second-hand Evidence. — Ignorance of the People. — The Difference now. — Reporters on the Ground, Witnesses in Court, etc., etc. — Bible Evidences through bad Hands. — Testimony of Lardner, Casaubon, Selmer, *et al.* — Lying for the glory of God. — Testimony of eminent Christians. — Internal Evidences. — Abraham chasing his Enemies four hundred Years into the Future. — An old Boy. — That flock of Quails. — Samson jawing the Philistines. — Those fiery-tailed Foxes. — Can the Bible stand before its own Guns. — Did Samuel, Moses, and Elijah come back? — Bible can not be true and Spiritualism false. — Living Witnesses. — The Walls of Jericho. — A Dialogue... 38

CHAPTER III.

TEACHINGS OF THE BIBLE AND SPIRITUALISM.

The Boast of Christians. — Age of the Bible no Argument in its favor. — A few knotty Questions. — Author does not dispute the Designs of Christianity. — Testimonies of Christians on the failure of Christianity. — Christians accuse each other. — Paul in a Dilemma. — His Plan of Escape. — Confessions of modern Christians. — Jesus' Parables leading in the wrong Direction. — The prodigal Son. — The unjust Steward. — Jesus commends the Scoundrel. — The unjust Judge. — Reasons for Prayer. — The Laborers in the Vineyard. — Does God play the same Game. — Bad Precepts. — Borrowing of the Egyptians. — Children of Israel not Slaves in Egypt. — What to do with bad Meat. — Punishment for religious Differences. — Treatment of bad Boys. — The Bible on Slavery. — On the treatment of Slaves. — The war upon the Midianites. — Biblical Temperance. — Sketches from Jesus' Sermon. — Jesus a disturber of domestic Relations. — A cool Reception. — Immoral Doctrines. — Works of no avail. — Character of the biblical God — The Difference. — The *modus operandi* of Salvation. — Proper Generation *vs.* Regeneration. — Recipe for making Hogs of Children. — How to cure Depravity. — Rest when Nature rests; work when she works. — North and South ends of People. — Ten syllogistic Arguments. — Conclusion............... 54

CHAPTER IV.

THE MISSION OF SPIRITUALISM.

Spiritualism necessarily iconoclastic. — A superior Light. — Jesus *vs.* Moses. — The World's Light and Saviours. — Relation of Spiritualism to Christianity. — The Decay of Institutions. — Babylon, Greece, Rome. — Republicanism as it was and is. — All stationary Institutions doomed. — The Good of all preserved. — A moving World. — A Glance at the Christian World. — "What went ye out for to see." — A lethargic State. — The Infidel World. — A Feast of Negatives. — Dominion of Orthodoxy. — Programme changed. — Ministers on their good Behavior. — A Thought-awakener. — The Hydesville Manifestations. — The *Vox Populi*. — Table Tippings. — New Theories of Explanation. — Writing Mediumship. — A new Set of Thoughts awakened. — Entrancement. — Sublimity of the Subject. — Efforts to confound the Media. — Opposers confounded. — A Change of Base. — A new Element of Success. — A Hearing obtained. — Number of its Adherents. — Elements of Success. — Not a Matter of Faith. — Quality of Spiritualists. — Their Happiness. — Questions for Skeptics. — Death and the Grave destroyed. — An outside Work. — A few Words with Spiritualists. — A Bid for your Spiritualism. — Our Duty. 101

CHAPTER V.

THE CUI BONO OF SPIRITUALISM.

A proper Inquiry. — Its Work slow. — Jesus' Argument. — "By their Fruits shall ye know them." — Author's Experience. — A Struggle with Poverty. — Letter from Dr. Newton. — Reflections on the Same. — Author takes Courage. — Dr. Newton's Three Months' Work. — Suicide of a Girl. — Her dead Mother kept her from Sin. — Worldly Good of Spiritualism. — Serfs liberated. — Lizzie Keizer and the Apple Peddler. — Experience as a Healer. — Cure of a withered Hand. — A Lady saved. — That Bread Fund. — A Medium saved from a Railroad Accident. — A Train of Cars saved by Spirit Interposition. — Peter West saves a Train of Cars. — A Collision avoided. — A Conflagration saved by Spirits. — Pair of Shoes sent to a Beggar. — Inventions by Spirits. — Moral Good of Spiritualism. — A Methodist Lady in Trouble. — A Dialogue. — Petty Tyranny. — A Drunkard saved. — A Case in Wisconsin. — Case in Chicago. — Spirits curing Appetite for Tobacco. — A Medium compelled to restore his ill-gotten Money. — Other Stimulants to Purity. — "Be sure your Sins will find you out." — Mental good of Spiritualism. — Lady saved from Insanity by her Spirit Son. — Asylums cheated out of Subjects. — Case in Iowa. — Only a few Grains. — Spiritualism in a dying Hour. 122

CHAPTER VI.

MINOR QUESTIONS.

Asking and answering Questions, the difference. — Can not answer every Question. — Spiritualism necessarily crude at first. — May be modified. — How do Spirits operate? — Their Power over the Will. — Does Mediumship indicate a weak Mind. — The controlling Spirit not necessarily with the Medium. — Author's Experiments. — Spirits control more than One at a time. — Sometimes control without knowing it. — A. J. Davis and Professor Vaughan. — "Arabula" and "Human Nature." — E. D. Keene gives a Communication from a Man yet on Earth. — Why do Spirits lie? — Fault often in the Medium. — Psychological Experiments. — Cause of Failure. — Reason why some get better Tests than others. — Why do not all Mediums give Tests. — Tests not always from personal Friends. — Psychology and Spiritualism. — All are Mediums. — David and his Mediums. — Philosophy of Dark Circles. — Biblical Manifestations in the Dark. — The Explanation. — Morality of Spiritualism. — Mediumship a Quickener. — Spiritualism and Sunshine. — Webster, Clay, *et al.*, whittled down. — The Explanation. — How to receive Spiritualism. — Why so many Indian Spirits. — The Indian Element positive. — Belongs in this Country. — Better Magnetizers. — More easily imitated Humbugs and the Self-deceived. — Experience of the Author. — Where are the Ancients. — Reasons why they do not return. — What Good can Spiritualism do? — For what should we go to Spirits. — Demonstrates a Future. — What will Science do? — Spiritual Sense. — Immortality Triumphant. . 151

CHAPTER VII.

ACTS OF THE APOSTLES AND SPIRITUALISM.

An interesting Book. — Then and now, the Analogy. — A solemn Warning. — Skepticism of the Disciples. — "Infallible Proof." — Better Manifestations To-day. — The waiting Time. — The Promise. — What is the Comforter? — Jesus' coming. — The Holy Ghost. — The two Men. — Synopsis of Acts II. — The Cripple healed. — How it was done. — Peter in Court. — Admissions of his Adversaries. — House and Furniture shaken. — Ananias and Sapphira. — Shadow Cures. — The Same now. — Case in St. Louis. — Apostles imprisoned. — Liberated by Spirits. — Report of the Committee. — A modern Case. — A "Mysterious Man." — Stephen's Sermon. — Stephen a Clairvoyant. — Assassination of Stephen. — Peter as a developing Medium. — Simon does not understand the Matter. — Philip a Medium. — Angels talk to him. — A Spirit carries him away. — Author carried by Spirits. — Another Case. — A new Star. 174

CHAPTER VIII.

MORE OF THE SAME.

Saul of Tarsus. — A good Manifestation. — The Points stated. — Ananias a Medium. — Did Paul see Jesus? — Another Case of Healing. — Reanimation of Dorcas. — Cornelius's Vision. — A Test. — Peter's Entrancement. — Another Test. — Angel, Spirit, Man. — Peter's preaching. — Spirits eating and drinking. — A second Edition of Pentecost. — Peter's Defence before his Jewish Brethren. — Agabus prophesies under Spirit Power. — Peter released by Spirits. — Particulars of the Case. — Peter at the Gate, his Angel. — Is this true? — Elymas's psychological Blindness. — Paul on the Appearance of Jesus. — Paul heals a Cripple. — Narrative of Paul and Barnabas. — Who is the Man of Macedonia? — Who is the Lord? — Paul and the female Medium. — Who was the Spirit cast out? — Paul and Silas let out of Jail. — Prison shaken and Bands fall off in the Dark. — Iron Rings removed. — Strange Gods. — Apotheosized Men. — Heathen Gods once Men. — Developing Circle at Ephesus. — "Handkerchiefs and Aprons." — A Minister denying his Bible. — The Spirits and the Sons of Sceva. — An Accident. — Paul prophesies. — Another Medium prophesies. — Paul relates his spiritual Experience. — Paul in a Trance. — Takes Sides with the Pharisees. — Communication to the Sailors. — A Ship saved by Spirits. — Among Barbarians. — A Snake Bite. — Success as a Healer. — A few Questions. — A word of Warning.......... 190

CHAPTER IX.

WHAT IS EVANGELICALISM.

A general Departure from Evangelicalism. — Bible on Infant Damnation. — The Gods of Orthodoxy. — Eternally begotten Son, meaning of. — Eternal Decrees. — Prayer and the Decrees. — Predestination and Reprobation. — Consequences of the Doctrine. — Presbyterian Justice. — The World made of Nothing in six Days. — The Fall of Man. — The Devil in the Snake. — All for God's Glory. — Adam totally depraved. — The Result. — Very God and very Man. — God his own Son and Father. — A naughty Ghost. — Mary God's Mother. — A Pyramid of Absurdities. — Justice satisfied. — No Power to will. — Who are the Called? — Elect Infants. — Doom of Non-professors. — Saved by Christ's Righteousness alone. — Is a second Payment demanded. — Catechisms on Punishment. — Sinfulness of Goodness. — Perseverance of the Saints. — Spiritualism, twenty of its Points of Superiority. — Conclusion............. 216

THE CONTRAST.

CHAPTER I.

WHAT IS SPIRITUALISM?

Author describes his own Spiritualism. — Division of the Subject. — Religion of Spiritualism. — Objections to the term Religion. — Ground of Objection. — First Ideas, God a Spirit. — Second, Man a Spiritual Being. — Is Man infinite. — " Communion of Saints." — Revelation not infallible. — Some Parts of the Bible more important than others. — " Cause and Cure of Infidelity." — Burgon on the Bible. — What Spiritualism denies. — Total Depravity. — Who believes it. — Chicago Fire and its Lesson. — Atonement weighed in the Balance. — Man in the Garden. — Clark on Genesis ii. 16. — Benson on Same. — Buck and the Confession of Faith on the Penalty. — " Spiritual Death " defined. — Badly mixed. — Adam and Eve in Court. — A foolish Judge. — Adam's Dialogue with Men and Devils. — An unjust Judge. — The Principle applied to our Courts. — Conditions of vicarious Atonement. — Did Jesus die a spiritual Death? — How can Man be vicariously redeemed from Hell? — Formal Worship and our Duty. — Shall we ask the Blessing? — The Time for Worship and Sabbaths. — Vocal Prayer. — Jesus on public Prayer. — The Brotherhood of Man and its Corollaries. — Our Duty to the Family. — Endless Progression. — Man the Author of his own Heavens and Hells. — No Infallibility even among the Good. — Spiritual Philosophy and Philosophy of Spiritualism. — Source of Power. — Philosophy of Entrancement. — The inward Monitor. — No perfect Standard. — Science of making People good. — Rules of Life developed out of Conditions. — The Treatment of Sin. — Should Consumptives and Cripples be hung. — History of Spiritualism everywhere. — A. J. Davis's Prophecy. — Rapid Advancement of the Cause. — Foretold Evils have not followed. — The present Work. — Concluding Suggestions.

It can not be expected that the question at the head of this chapter can be fully answered in one chapter, or even in an ordinary sized volume; yet a synopsis of Spiritualism can be so stated in a single chapter that the reader can get an idea of its general features. Its panorama can be so unrolled that the observer can get enough of a view to decide whether it is worth the time it would take to go into a more thorough analysis of its *minutiæ*.

I do not propose in this volume to be unnecessarily responsible for the general belief or practice of the great family of Spiritualists, nor are they responsible for anything I shall say or do. I can only, in my writings and actions, represent the Spiritualism of a single individual; I shall therefore proceed to explain my own Spiritualism.

In making the outlines of Spiritualism I shall divide it into four parts. I will consider, —

1. Its Religion.
2. Its Philosophy.
3. Its Morals.
4. Its History.

THE RELIGION OF SPIRITUALISM.

I use the term Religion, especially when I apply it to Spiritualism, in an accommodated sense. Strictly considered, it is a term I do not like; it was invented to imply the restoration of man from the fall. It implies original sin, total depravity, and all its *et ceteras*. The term religion is a compound of two Latin words, *re* and *ligo*, signifying to *re-bind*, or bind again. As I never was unbound or cut loose from God, I need no re-binding. I never participated in any man's fall, much less that of old father Adam, therefore have no part or lot in his restoration. When, however, the term religion is used in the sense of theology, or an effort to know and practice every duty, to arise daily to a purer and better life, Spiritualists are religious. Permit me, then, when I use the term religion in this chapter, to use it in this accommodated sense.

The first idea in my spiritual theology is that, "God is a Spirit;" or rather, that God is spirit; for I never like to put a definite or indefinite article before the three letters, G-O-D. I would like the phraseology quite as well, and it would be equally as true, if it was reversed, so as to read, "Spirit is God."

The next basic fact of Spiritualism is that man is a spiritual being, possessing all the attributes that belong to spirit anywhere. God has no attribute with which man is not endowed. Many of man's attributes and much of his power may be *latent*. Yet man has in *germ* all there is in the universe. Some do not know this, others do not believe it; yet all recognize that they have powers to-day that they could not have used one year since. The fact is, you have no power to-day that was not born with you. It has taken all these years to develop and bring into activity the amount of power you now have. Man never has reached the *Ultima Thule* in any direction: that being the case, if there is an ultimatum, he does not know it.

Does the objector urge that, though man has not circumnavigated, weighed, measured, and found the limits of his powers, he *may* yet find them? I answer, the same applies to God. How does the God power know but that some time it may find a power too much for it? When this question is answered, I will apply the answer to the spirit of man, which is the repository of infinite possibilities.

As two drops of water find an affinity for each other and intermingle, as oil blends with oil, so spirit, wherever it may be, blends with spirit. As spirits out of the body may blend with each other, and spirits in the body may blend with each other, so spirits out of the body and spirits in the body may interblend. The reader is by this time ready to understand that the first definite article in the spiritualistic faith is the doctrine of the communion of saints.

Believing that under the proper conditions spirit can communicate with spirit, in either world, they of course believe in not only a daily, but, if necessary, a *continuous* revelation from spirits. All Spiritualists must therefore believe in inspiration and revelation; yet they do not believe that any revelation is plenarily or infallibly inspired. Infallible inspiration to a fallible being is an impossibility.

All revelation partakes more or less of the nature of that through which it comes; hence, until media can be absolutely perfect in their physical organisms, the manifestations given through mediumship must be more or less imperfect. Water sometimes tastes of the vessel in which it is kept. Light always partakes of the color of the glass through which it comes. The mediums who wrote the Bible were certainly inspired, yet the inspiration could not prevent the writers' manifesting their own idiosyncrasies; hence, even the Bible, though the work of inspiration, lacks a great deal of being perfect. A little reflection will convince any reasoner of the truth of this proposition.

The most profound Bible believer regards some parts of the Bible as being more sacred and important than others; but there can be no degrees in perfection;

therefore the Bible is not perfect. Who admires David's cursing psalm (the CIXth) as they do the XIXth or XXIId? Reader, I appeal to you, if you were compelled to see some portions of the Bible annihilated, and could have your choice as to which you would yield, would you find any trouble in deciding whether to retain the Lord's Sermon or the history of the love affair between Boaz and Ruth? Which do you prefer, the Song of Solomon or the Lord's Prayer? The very fact that you could make a choice is proof that you do not regard the Bible as absolutely infallible. I now submit that you agree with the Spiritualists that the Bible, though inspired, is not an infallible revelation from God. All the inspiration of the spirit world could not spoil Paul's education or logic, nor yet make an educated man or logician of Peter. His brain was not the kind that could be inspired in that way.

Occasionally one hears the idea advanced that the Bible is infallible; but such cases are more rare than in former days. Rev. David Nelson, nearly a half century since, wrote a work entitled "the Cause and Cure of Infidelity"—a work, by the way, which, I think, has caused more infidelity than it ever cured; in that he states that "every sentence and every *part* of a sentence of the Bible is plenarily inspired and infallibly true."

Rev. Mr. Burgon, a later writer, says, "The Bible is none other than *the voice of Him* that sitteth upon the throne! Every book of it, every chapter of it, every word of it, every syllable of it, *every letter of it* [Good Heavens! won't the man permit us to drop out just one letter?] is the direct utterance of the Most High! The Bible is none other than the word of

God — not some part of it more, some part of it less, but all alike, — the utterance of Him who sitteth upon the throne — absolute, faultless, unerring, supreme."

The Rev. who penned the above doubtlessly would prize the obscene story of Onan, or Ezekiel's bread receipt, as highly as he would the "Golden Rule," or the first and greatest commandment. It is only occasionally that such fossils are met with. There are but few now who even think they believe in the absolute perfection of the Bible. A great majority of the most devout Christians now recognize that the character of each biblical writer is indicated in his writings. Thus any one who would read the Song of Solomon would need no statement as to the number of his wives and concubines for intelligent readers could not help but know that the number would only be limited by his ability to obtain them.

Spiritualism in its dogmas is not purely affirmative; it denies as well. Believing as it does that man is the offspring of the Most High, — that spirit sprang from spirit, — it necessarily denies the old church doctrine of original sin and consequent total depravity. It knows no one so low, morally or intellectually, but that there is a divinity within him or her which will some time assert itself. I am by this subject as I am by that of inspiration; I doubt whether one who allows himself to think on it can differ with Spiritualists, much less argue an opposite side of the question. It is possible that an individual, while reading *Buck's Theological* Dictionary, may for the moment conclude that man is so totally depraved that he can not do a good act, speak a good word, or think a good thought, unless especially aided by power from on high; but such belief can only last a few seconds after the volume is laid aside.

No mother ever yet pointed to her own unconverted child as a specimen of total depravity. No theologian will point to his own son, however wicked he may be, and say, " There is no good in him." Such calamities as the fire that consumed Chicago in 1871 afford an unanswerable argument against the dogma. That terrible calamity developed the fact that all — even theater actors, to whom the ministry had ever pointed as especial arguments in favor of the necessity of men and women being made better — had divine natures, which as spontaneously went out in words and deeds in behalf of the suffering, as was manifest in any church in the land. The late James Fisk, whom almost every editor and preacher in the land had denounced as being a sinner above all others, had a noble quality, which in this instance responded to the prayers of sufferers in a ten thousand dollar check. When such men as A. T. Stewart, of New York, count out fifty thousand dollars to help the sufferers of a single calamity, and railroad kings grant the free and unlimited use of their roads to two hundred thousand sufferers, I can not for one moment admit that they are totally depraved. Even the Heathen Chinee, in the " Golden State," who have suffered more from the depravity of Christians than Christians ever have from heathens, magnanimously stepped forward and contributed thirteen thousand dollars to relieve the sufferings of their Christian brethren.

Spiritualism, rejecting in toto the idea of the fall of man, has no use for an atonement. It does not believe that man has ever been separated from God, therefore has no need to be made at one with him. Spiritualists generally regard the doctrine of the atonement not only as untrue, but as pernicious in its tendencies. Could they believe in an atonement at all, they could not believe in one based on vicarious suffering. It is said by Christians that Jesus suffered the penalty due for man's transgression, and in that made man at one with God, that is, placed him where he was before the fall. I know of no better way to explain this than to look after the results of the fall, as explained by Christians, and then apply Jesus' suffering and the atonement, and see the result.

Man, according to the theories which see so much evil in Spiritualism, was made of dust, about six thousand years since, and placed in a garden, where everything was beautiful and good except one tree, that may have been both beautiful to the eye and pleasant to the taste; yet there was either something intrinsically poison in the fruit, or man for eating it was arbitrarily condemned. At least man was solemnly warned against eating the fruit, which warning he did not heed. The result is, according to orthodoxy, death, spiritual, temporal, and eternal death. Dr. Clarke says, —

"*Thou shalt surely die. Moth tamuth;* literally, *a death thou shalt die;* or *dying thou shalt die.* Thou shalt not only die spiritually, by losing the life of God, but from that moment thou shalt become mortal." — *Clarke's Com. on Gen.* ii. 16.

"The death here threatened is evidently to be considered as opposed to the life (or lives, rather) which God has bestowed on him. This was not only the natural life of his body, in its union with his soul, but the *spiritual life of his soul* in its union with God, and the eternal life of both. The threatening then implies, Thou shalt not only lose all the happiness thou hast, either in possession or in prospect, and be liable to the death of the body, and all the miseries which precede and accompany it, but thou shalt lose thy spiritual life and become dead to God — dead to God and things divine, and shalt even *forfeit thy title to immortality*, and be liable to death eternal, and all this *in the day thou eatest thereof.*" — *Benson's Com.*

"*The covenant of works* was made with Adam; the condition of which was his perseverance during the whole time of his probation. The reward annexed to his obedience was the continuance of him and his posterity in such perfect holiness and felicity as he then had, while upon earth, and an everlasting life with God hereafter. The *penalty* threatened for the breach of the commandment was condemnation, terminating in death, temporal, spiritual, and eternal." — *Buck's Theological Dictionary*, under "*Covenant of Works.*"

The Westminster Confession of Faith, pp. 45, 46, says, —

"Every sin, both original and eternal, being a transgression of the righteous law of God, and contrary thereunto, doth in its own nature bring guilt upon the sinner, whereby he is bound over to the wrath of God and curse of the law, and so made subject to death, with miseries, spiritual, temporal, and eternal."

Spiritual death they have defined to be a continuation in sin, a loss of all desire to do good, or, in other words, *total depravity*. This subject I have considered in a former part of this chapter; yet I should feel that I had neglected my duty were I not to devote a few more words to it, considering it in the light of a penalty for the Adamic sin.

The system of religion styling itself Orthodoxy, though inconsistent on many points, rather overdoes itself on this. A loss of the desire to do good, which is defined to be spiritual death, and hence a part of the penalty of the Adamic law, must precede, and not follow, the transgression. It would puzzle even a doctor of divinity to tell how a man could willfully and deliberately transgress a law until he had lost the desire to obey! The consent of the mind must be obtained before the body would voluntarily act in that direction. Hence Adam must have lost the desire to obey while he was pure and holy, before he transgressed; that being the case, spiritual death was the *cause*, and not the penalty, of the Adamic sin.

Spiritual death is defined to be simply a state of depravity, or being under the dominion of sin.

Buck says, —

"Spiritual death is that awful state of ignorance, insensibility, and disobedience, which mankind are in by nature, and which excludes them from the favor and enjoyment of God." — *Theological Dictionary.*

Permit me for a moment to suppose this to be a truth, and the whole allegory of the transgression in the Garden of Eden to be a literal fact. The circumstance would run something like this: "Adam and Eve transgressed, and are arraigned for trial, and called into court. After a full confession of their guilt the Judge proceeds to pronounce the penalty, that is, that they shall be sinners, — greater sinners, — totally depraved. That is as if a judge should say to a horse thief, "From your confession, I perceive that you have stolen a horse. I pronounce as a penalty that you shall be a horse thief." Should the idea suggest itself to the culprit that horse stealing was the *crime*, and not the penalty, the judge would proceed to explain. "Sir, I perceive that you do not understand this penalty. I do not mean that it shall always remain a fact that you have stolen a horse, for that fact may, by a peculiar process, be blotted out; but I do mean that you shall continue to steal horses. You shall be so totally given up to kleptomania that you will find it utterly impossible to resist the impulse to steal." Reader, what would you think of such an explanation of the penalty of horse stealing? How foolish does the orthodox explanation make the God of the Bible, when it makes depravity the result of sin!

The absurdity of this has not yet reached its climax. Temporal or physical death, we are informed, is another portion of the penalty of Adam's sin. Suppose, according to this sentiment, that Adam and Eve go on for nearly nine hundred years, *enjoying* depravity, which is the penalty of depravity; at the end of that time old father Adam finds that his locks have turned as white as the driven snow, his hearing has grown thick, his eyes dim, his limbs paralyzed, and his breath short. Something is wrong; he does not know what it is, but for some cause his body refuses to perform its functions. His sons and daughters gather around his bed and make the announcement, "Father, you are dying!" "What, dying!" says the old man. "Yes, physically dying." "Why is this?" inquires the expiring Adam. "Why," responds the son, "don't you remember the circumstance of eating the forbidden fruit? The penalty was, 'In the day thou eatest thereof thou shalt surely die.'" "I well remember that," says the dying man, "but I have paid the penalty for that sin. I died a spiritual death in the very day I transgressed." "But," responds the son, "you ought to have had a spiritual birth; it would have enabled you to have understood that the law *meant* that you should have died two kinds of death for that sin." The poor, dying man has only strength left to say, "Why did not the law express its meaning in unmistakable language?" and expires.

Every rational creature will join with him and say, "Adam, your complaints are just. This God is a tyrant in inflicting a penalty not mentioned in the law. If God meant you should die more than once, he should have said so."

Poor Adam's spirit leaves the body, hoping that with him this is the last of the consequences of having eaten the forbidden fruit; but he hardly finds himself in the world of spirits, ere devils gather around him to drag him down to dark despair. They take him to the sulphurous regions, and as they unbar the door, and let the flames and smoke burst into his face, he inquires the meaning of this. He is answered, "This is death — eternal death." "And must I suffer this?" inquires Adam; "and for what?" He is again informed of his sin in Eden. Adam expostulates with the powers that be, pleading that he has already twice suffered the penalty for that sin; but all to no purpose. He is answered, "God's ways are not as your ways," and plunged into a gulf of dark despair, to suffer, gnash his teeth, and gnaw his white-hot chains to all eternity.

Suppose our courts were to act on the principle that orthodoxy represents God as adopting, with reference to man's sin. The law says the penalty for *petty larceny* shall be confinement in the county jail for a period of time not exceeding thirty days. Neighbor A., having no money, and being hungry, steals a loaf of bread. He is caught, tried, found guilty, and sentenced to the jail. After remaining there the time allotted by the law, the proper officer comes to take him out. As A. is being conducted out of the jail, he says, " Well, I have violated your law and paid the penalty." " O, no," says the officer, " we are not done with you yet. You must now go to the state's prison, and be confined to hard labor for five years." " What! Imprison me? and for what?" says A. " For stealing a loaf of bread," responds the officer. " But the law does not say so," says A. " It means it," is the reply. And poor A. is sent to the state's prison.

At the end of five years the proper officer again approaches A., to release him. " There," says A., " I have broken your law, and paid two penalties for it; are you now done with me?" " No, sir," says the officer; " you must now be hanged by the neck, until you are dead." A., startled and amazed, asks what he is to be hanged for? He is again referred to the loaf of bread, and told that the penalty for *petty larceny*, when rightly interpreted, means all that has been and is to be inflicted on him. Now I ask, in all candor, would not every rational being in the world rebel at such a procedure? Yet these are the lessons orthodoxy teaches us of God.

Am I answered that this is not a full statement;

that though we do believe in this moral, temporal, and eternal death, we believe, also, in the *vicarious* suffering of Jesus, which brings man out, if he will, from under all these penalties! Is that so?

The meaning of the word *vicarious*, is one suffering the penalty of the law instead of another. No one believes that the vicarious sufferings of Jesus entirely relieve the sinner from the consequence of sin. The most that is claimed is, that it reclaims and brings out from under spiritual and physical death, and saves from the other third of the penalty, which is eternal death, or rather eternal suffering. Thus, in order for Jesus to redeem man from spiritual death, or total depravity, he must endure the same, and have a spiritual resurrection, or be converted. Did Jesus pass through this? If not, vicarious suffering fails at the start, as Jesus did not endure it. If he did, "the wages of sin is death," and hence Jesus will have all he can do to die for his own sins, and not for those of Adam or the world. Supposing, however, that the vicarious sufferings of Jesus had redeemed man from spiritual death, his work is even then only one third done. Now man is to be redeemed from physical death: that is to be done, we are told, by Jesus' experiencing the same on the cross, and rising from the dead. Admitting all this to be accomplished, the worst is still to come. Man is to be vicariously redeemed from an eternal hell. This of course can be done in no other way than by Jesus suffering the same. Thus, instead of an atonement, the logical sequence of orthodoxy is, that Christ and the whole human family must endure eternal torture in a lake of fire and brimstone.

The foregoing, with many other similar reasons, together with an entire absence of proof of the fall of man and the atonement, are sufficient reasons for the Spiritualists' denials of the essentials of orthodoxy.

Among the orthodox doctrines that Spiritualism denies, is its whole system of formal or ceremonial worship. Some even go so far as to think that if the whole system of forms and ceremonies was abolished, " the world would be the better for it." Spiritualists generally conceive that if there was not so much importance attached to the baptisms, the eucharist, and other church ordinances, there would be more room to attach importance to real spiritual and intellectual development; that if people did not study forms so much, they would study *duties* more; that it is more our duty to see that widows and orphans are cared for, that the wants of the sick are relieved, than that certain hours are set apart to pray, or observe as holy time.

Many evangelical Christians ask a blessing or return thanks every time they sit down to their meals. Spiritualists believe that good, healthy food, taken in proper quantities and at proper times, is a blessing to the partaker, without any words being said over it. Improper food, or food taken in improper quantities, or at improper hours, can not be sanctified to the use of those who partake. The partaking of it is a curse. No God would dare to bless it. It would be setting an example which would ruin the world with dyspepsia, liver complaint, and gout. The fact that orthodox Christians are as likely to be troubled with all these complaints as are infidels and Spiritualists, proves their blessings to be only " as sounding brass or tinkling cymbal."

Spiritualists can not see why a formal blessing should be asked any more over each meal, than over every drink of water or every apple or nut eaten between meals; or why people should not, upon the same principle, go through the same ceremony at their bedside, their chopping, blacksmithing, or dish-washing. The fact is, while it is always proper to be reverential to all there is above and beyond us; and aspiring toward the good, the pure, and the beautiful, these foolish stated ceremonies, while they clothe one with the appearance or form of godliness, so effectually clip the wings of true devotion, that they destroy the power thereof. Any forms or ceremonies that compel their adherents to bow to them for fashion's sake, must more or less stultify the natural outgushing of the same. It must be confessed that often while the lips are saying prayers or singing praises the heart is on business, or somewhere else, as far from the service of the lips as the poles are from each other.

Spiritualists believe the proper time to eat is when one is hungry, the proper time to rest or *sabbatize* is when one is tired; so the proper time to pray is when the spirit of prayer comes, and at no other time. Then pray, whether in an audience chamber, a machine shop, or a brick yard. Withdraw your person from the crowd if convenient; if not, retire into your soul's secret closet, and there commune with the higher spiritual life. As prayer is purely an aspiration, no vocal words need, as a general thing, be used. If prayer is for God's benefit, that he may know and be willing to redress our wants, certainly, God being spirit, reads our spirit and understands our requests without our framing them into words. Spiritualists generally think that the power we call God has an understanding of its business, therefore do not believe, to any great extent, in dictating what it shall and shall not do.

A prayer is a plea made; but a plea for Almighty God to do something, implies that the one making the plea either fears that God would neglect his duty, or that he wants something that God could not bestow without going outside of his duty. In one instance prayer implies that God is derelict in his duty, in the other that God is wanted to do something more than justice. Spiritualists do not generally believe that man could at present control matters very much by prayer, if he would; nor do they believe that the machinery of the universe would run much more smoothly if men controlled it all by their prayers.

Prayer before an audience is, as Jesus said, made to be heard of men. His words are, —

"And when thou prayest, thou shalt not be as the hypocrites are: for they love to pray standing in the synagogues and in the corners of the streets, that they may be seen of men. Verily I say unto you, They have their reward.

"But thou when thou prayest, enter into thy closet, and when thou hast shut thy door, pray to thy Father which is in secret; and thy Father which seeth in secret, shall reward thee openly." (Matt. vi. 5, 6.)

For one, I am perfectly willing that those who regard Jesus as one third of the Infallible Deity, may violate these words: I must obey them. When I pray before an audience, let it be understood I am like others: I pray to be heard of men. Prayer is the birth pangs of new desires, new aspirations, new inspirations; the proper place for it is in the secret closet. When the spirit of prayer comes, be sure it is the precursor of something good. Go to your secret closet in the dark if possible, shut everything external away from you, then open your heart, your aspirations, your soul. Under these circumstances the angel within you and angels without can come nearer together, and soul will commune with souls more perfectly than under other conditions.

Spiritualism, believing as it does that man is a spiritual being, and that all sprang from the fountain of spirit called God, can not believe otherwise than in the brotherhood of man, however far back we may be compelled to find the evidence of that brotherhood: all are streams from the same great fountain. Believing this doctrine, of course they can not believe in any practice, nor consistently practice any belief that would be contrary to these sentiments. Lawsuits, quarrels, fights, slavery, war, or neighbor lying to or cheating neighbor, is not brotherly. Spiritualists can but be opposed to such things. This doctrine of brotherhood should, when carried to its legitimate extent, go farther than to teach us what we should *not* do to each other: it should teach us positive duties to each other. If all men and women are my brothers and sisters, then I am under obligation to do the duty of a brother by all, — to help the weak and unfortunate, to relieve the suffering, and as far as in me lies, to see that each has justice in all things. Men are sometimes inclined to trample on each other. Reader, do you realize that the crushed and the one who crushes are both your brothers? Have you no duties in such cases? That woman in the brothel, whom you call fallen, is your sister, as much so as the most pious lady on earth. One of our elder brothers, Jesus, said to one such, "Neither do I condemn thee: go and sin no more." Will you consider her a sister, and say the same? You have duties here. Once more. When about to lead a young man into a gambling hell or a drinking saloon, or a young woman into a house of assignation, think this is my brother or sister. I am, as a stronger brother, bound in honor for his or her *protection* — not destruction; such thoughts should turn you from your evil purpose.

In passing judgment upon those called sinners, try to think of such as brothers and sisters, — weak, sickly brothers and sisters, —" flesh of your flesh, and bone of your bone." More than all, spirit of your spirit — of God's spirit. Consider yourself, least you should also be tempted.

> " This life is a play, where each human heart,
> To make the *denouement*, must act out its part.
> If all men, like sheep, would follow one way,
> Then life would indeed be a very poor play.
> 'Tis a law of our being, most pointedly shown,
> That each soul must live out a life of his own.
> Ah! be not too rash to judge of another,
> But ever remember that man is your brother.
> God made the owl see where man's sight is dim,
> And the light that guides you may be darkness to him!
> 'Tis a great truth to learn, — a prize if you win it, —
> There's room in the world for all that is in it."

Following the thought of the brotherhood of man, in Spiritualism is that of endless progression. There are very few outside of the ranks of Spiritualists who believe this doctrine, and those who do are hardly able to tell why, much less to demonstrate the groundwork of that faith. According to Spiritualism, man enters the next world just where he leaves this, surrounded by the conditions that he has made for himself by his words and acts in this world, and then in the other world goes on making his own misery or happiness by his conduct.

Man is now, and will eternally be, what he makes himself. Heaven and hell are both latently within every one. God will not go out of his way to put any one into happiness or misery. The fuel, the kindling-wood, and the match that lights the fires of hell, are within every one; and if ever the fires of hell are ignited, the sinner himself will do the incendiary work, and take the consequences.

Spiritualism does not allow that any one, even in heaven, is infallible. Those called good can, in the spirit world as in this, make mistakes; and the bad are not wholly bad. There is no absolute perfection in the universe: man always has, and ever will improve. Here it may be well to close the argument on the religion of Spiritualism. Should I devote as much time to each department of this chapter as I have to this, it would swell itself to a volume. I now pass to a consideration of the

PHILOSOPHY OF SPIRITUALISM.

Two widely different things are often sadly confounded: one is the Philosophy of Spiritualism, the other is the Spiritual Philosophy. By the latter phrase, Spiritualists mean the general laws or principles taught in or drawn out of Spiritualism. By the former, they mean the general laws or principles by which the various spiritual phenomena are produced.

Permit me first, in this division of the subject, to speak of general spirit intercourse. All volition or power inheres in spirit. I move the pen with which I now write, by moving the bones of my hand; these bones are moved by the muscle, the muscle is moved by the blood, the blood is driven by the electric currents which pass from the brain through the nerves; these currents are set in motion by the spirit. Thus the writing of this book, and in fact every motion of the hand, foot, or head, is a physical manifestation of spirit-power. Spirit can operate on nothing but spirit, or that which is next to it, which is electricity. When spirits move tables or chairs, or rap out answers to questions, they use only natural powers; they get control of the electrical currents there are in the room or around the table, and through them move ponderable substances.

Every nerve is a battery, through which spirit drives the electric current. Brain is but a congress of nerves, and therefore a stronger battery. Through these brain and nerve forces spirits can sometimes approach and move ponderable substances.

The philosophy of entrancement is much the same. The brain is a battery through which spirits, when they get it well charged, can approach mortals, and hand their thoughts to the external world. The power of mediumship is more the power to hold still and submit to extraneous influences, than anything else. Spirit control is the same, whether effected by a spirit out of the body or in the body. In another chapter the reader will find that I have more fully discussed the philosophy of Spiritualism, explaining the necessity for darkness in order to produce certain manifestations; also, I have offered a few thoughts on the general conditions of spirit manifestations. I now pass to consider

THE MORALS OF SPIRITUALISM.

There is no question on which there exists greater differences of opinion than on this. It is true that Spiritualism, to some extent, ignores old traditions, authorities, and standards. It is also true that old ideas of morality, unless they have something more than age to recommend them, are below par among some of the Spiritualists. This is enough to cause certain persons, who borrow their ideas of right from the past, to see all the evidence that could possibly be required to prove that Spiritualism is leading the people away from virtue's paths. There are people in the world who could not be convinced that ancient landmarks can be departed from without ignoring every rule of right, and having a general chaos ensue. With others, there seems an actual necessity of departing from the old, as it has, after eighteen centuries of experience and effort, failed to make moral men and women of even its own adherents. Spiritualists have, many of them, noted the slavery, war, drunkenness, murder, burglary, and licentiousness yet in the world, and often practiced under the very steeples of the churches, and sometimes by ministers who occupy the pulpits. This occasionally causes one to say, as many more think, There is a radical wrong somewhere; Christianity, as a system, has failed to make the world good. Thus investigation has led them to conclude that Christianity has too nearly ignored or rejected the inward monitor; that if people had been looking within more, instead of to outside standards of right, and had striven to more thoroughly cultivate the acquaintance of the internal monitor, and developed good from within, working it out into every day practice, the world would to-day have been nearer heaven. Hence Spiritualism, if it has not already done so, must in a measure reject outside authorities with regard to right and wrong. In fact, until man is absolutely perfect, there can be no universal and infallible standard of right and wrong. It is acknowledged on all hands that man is more or less the creature of circumstances. Thousands of the Christians to-day, who denounce others for not looking through their glasses, owe all their Christianity to the circumstance of their having been born and reared at the time and place, and under the circumstances that have in turn been regarded as blessings or curses. Had they been born in a Mohammedan country, and educated by Mohammedan parents and teachers, they would probably denounce "Christian dogs" as infidels, worthy of nothing better than a Mohammedan hell. When it is understood that all are not born and reared under the same circumstances, it will be understood that all can not be tried by the same standard. I doubt whether any one, after a little reflection, would hold an idiot as thoroughly responsible for an infringement on the rights of others as they would one of greater capacity. We are all responsible in proportion to our capacity and development. This being the case, when a man kills another, the blame, if there be any, lies back of the murderer: it goes at least as far back as the cause that made him such. Our courts are beginning to recognize this idea: scarcely a murderer is tried but an effort is made, often with success, to prove him insane. Every child has a right to demand of society a birth and rearing beyond that of a murderer: conditions that will preclude the possibility of murder. The crimes of the present generation point to the sins of the past, and those to the past, and so *ad infinitum*.

Believing this, Spiritualists generally doubt whether the world can be reformed by *precepts*. They argue that men now know better than they can do. Spiritualists are therefore trying to develop a philosophy, the carrying out of which will as naturally make man better as the spring showers and sun will quicken vegetation into germination. Spiritualists claim that a child, begotten by the proper parents (those whose union should produce children), and under proper conditions, can not possibly be as bad as one begotten and born under other conditions. Many of them claim that if a child is properly generated and reared, he needs no regeneration. A person raised in filth and on improper food can not, out of that, develop as pure rules of life, nor a practice of as pure precepts, as one well washed, who lives in the right kind of a house, breathes the right kind of air, sleeps in the right kind of beds, wears the right kind of clothing, and eats food calculated to develop the right kind of brain and muscle. Therefore, instead of denouncing sin and sinners, they are going to work to eradicate sin and *cure* sinners. Moral and mental disease should be made a *study*, and treated in a manner analagous to the treatment of physical disease. All who have followed me thus far, are prepared to hear me say, that our courts are no more justifiable in hanging a murderer than they would be in hanging a consumptive, hunchback, or paralytic.

If the foregoing argument is true, no book standard of right and wrong can be given, any more than a book should regulate how often the heart should beat, or how often its readers should sneeze or cough, or how many fits of ague he should have, and by what intervals they should be separated. One will take cold more frequently than another, in spite of all the books in the world; so the one born a kleptomaniac will steal more frequently than the one having no temptation in that direction. Books can not stop it.

HISTORY OF SPIRITUALISM.

The reader will not understand from the above heading that it is my design to go into the *minutiæ* of the history of the Spiritual movement. To do that would require a volume as large as Webster's large dictionary; besides, it is at this stage of its development quite an unnecessary work. The history of Spiritualism besides, in part at least, written in books, is so perfectly engraved on the minds of the readers of this volume, that but little need be said. The every-day occurrences of the spiritual phenomena, in almost every department of the globe, has given it such a wide-spread notoriety, that enough of its history is within easy reach of every one to answer the purpose of this book.

Modern spirit manifestations came into the world unsought and unheralded, except by A. J. Davis, the Poughkeepsie seer. As much as four years before the " Rochester knockings," he was laughed at and regarded as insane, for publishing that the spirit world and this world would soon come in communication with each other. In fulfillment of Mr. Davis's prophecy, Spiritualism came undesired and unwelcomed. With no preacher or press to advocate its claims, it immediately began to make converts, gathering among its adherents persons of every rank and station in life. Editors, ministers, lawyers, doctors, actors on the stage, in short, men from every rank and station in life, fell before this mighty power. Nothing has stayed or even retarded the onward march of this new conqueror of the world. It has not only proved its right to life by living and thriving through all opposition, but it has questioned the right of hoary-headed errors to longer stay the march of mind. The doctrines that have been examined in this chapter have slunk away before Spiritualism, as bats and owls retire before the rising sun.

Although Spiritualism has in some way interwoven itself into the every-day reading, thoughts and life of the great majority of the Christian world, besides making between ten and fifteen millions of out-and-out converts ; and although it has instilled itself into about all the literature, and almost everything else of the age, the evils that were prophesied by ministers and editors as sure to follow, have in no case ensued. Those who embrace the new religion, instead of becoming the lawless horde of religious and spiritual adventurers, that some had prophesied as being the inevitable result, settled down, attending to their own business, with an honor, integrity, and ability often excelling their evangelical neighbors.

Spiritual halls are now being built, lyceums founded, societies incorporated, Young People's Spiritual associations organized, libraries and reading-rooms opened, and in every instance well patronized. Thus Spiritualism is now, as never before, compelling the world to *feel* and acknowledge its power. With this increase of converts and societies, there is a commensurate increase of knowledge and zeal among older Spiritualists. Old societies that had measurably become " weary in well doing," are reorganizing and buckling on the harness anew. New and talented speakers are being called into the field, and mediums for every form of manifestation are being faster and more perfectly developed than ever before. Thus is Spiritualism rapidly writing its own history in the hearts and heads of the people. More perfectly and indelibly does Spiritualism do its own history making than could possibly be told by my poor pen, were I to devote volumes to the elucidation of the subject.

Patient reader, with this in some respects brief, and in others prolix outline of what Spiritualism is, I close this statement, hoping that you have so fallen in love with what has been described as Spiritualism, as to be induced to follow me through the remainder of this volume.

CHAPTER II.

COMPARATIVE EVIDENCE OF THE BIBLE AND SPIRITUALISM.

No necessary Antagonism. — Christian Arguments used for Spiritualism. — Nicodemus's Argument. — The Works of Jesus and Mediums compared. — Did Jesus raise the Dead? — Modern Resurrections. — Testimony of Daily Papers. — A man resuscitated after having been buried ten Months. — Mrs. Lancaster resurrected. — Resurrection of Rev. William Tennent. — Jesus did not always succeed. — The healing at Bethesda only one of a thousand. — Why did he not heal others? — The Pentecostal Evidences considered. — Same in Spiritualism. — Suicidal Argument against Spiritualism. — Silly Spiritualism and the Bible compared. — Jesus eating Fish and Spirits eating Apples. — "Devils and Darkness" of Bible Times. — Biblical Evidence not conclusive. — Second-hand Evidence. — Ignorance of the People. — The Difference now. — Reporters on the Ground, witnesses in Court, etc.. etc. Bible Evidences through bad Hands. — Testimony of Lardner, Casaubon, Selmer, *et al.* — Lying for the glory of God. — Testimony of eminent Christians. — Internal Evidences. — Abraham chasing his Enemies four hundred Years into the Future. — An old Boy. — That flock of Quails. — Samson jawing the Philistines. — Those fiery-tailed Foxes. — Can the Bible stand before its own Guns. — Did Samuel, Moses, and Elijah come back? — Bible can not be true and Spiritualism false. — Living Witnesses. — The Walls of Jericho. — A Dialogue.

THOSE who oppose the inauguration of the Spiritual dispensation, do not seem to have ever been able to comprehend that a person could believe both the Bible and Spiritualism. Let a person announce himself a Spiritualist, and he is at once set down by its opposers as having totally rejected the Bible. Those acquainted with the opposition can not fail to have observed that in lectures, books, and essays against Spiritualism there has ever been an effort to create the impression that one embracing Spiritualism must necessarily have rejected the Bible. While such is not the case, I must confess that if I could not receive the truths and divinity of both — if I should be compelled to yield one or the other, the evidence of the truth and divinity of the Bible does not impress me as being so forcible as that of Spiritualism.

Individually I had much rather be permitted to choose the good of each, without any reference to the other. I can not see why Spiritualism should necessarily be evil or false because the Bible is good and true, nor can I understand how or why a reception of the truths of Spiritualism should involve a rejection of those taught in the Bible. Now, without any disparagement to the Bible or its contents, I propose to gratify the opposers of Spiritualism by a brief comparison of the evidences of the two systems. I know of no better way to commence this comparison than with the following proposition, viz. : —

THE ARGUMENTS USED IN FAVOR OF THE BIBLE APPLY WITH ALL THEIR FORCE TO MODERN SPIRITUALISM.

One of the first and most general arguments used in favor of the Bible and its chief hero, is that of Nicodemus, in John iii. 2. "Rabbi, we know that thou art a teacher come from God: for no man can do these miracles that thou doest, except God be with him." It is claimed that Nicodemus was a member of the Jewish Sanhedrim, and probably went as a representative of that body. He did not say *I* think, or *I* know, but *we* know that thou art a teacher come from God, etc. Thus he expresses either the faith of the Jewish senate, whose committee he was, or that of the nation. The argument is that Jesus' miracles were sufficient to call out the universal and unequivocal confession that he was a divinely sent teacher. If the Jews, his bitterest enemies, acknowledged his miracles, they must have occurred, and if they did occur, they prove the divinity of the religious system they were wrought to maintain. Thus by a "short method" is the Christian system lumped off, and proved of divine origin.

Now, I do not know of a Spiritualist who objects to this first argument for Christianity. We are perfectly willing it shall stand; all we ask is, that if the same reasons be found for believing in Spiritualism, they have the same weight in proving its divinity. Permit me to compare the works of Jesus and the early Christians with those of modern spirit mediums. The clearest statement of Jesus' works is made by himself in Matt. xi. 5: "The blind receive their sight, and the lame walk, the lepers are cleansed, and the deaf hear, the dead are raised up, and the poor have the gospel preached to them. And blessed is he whosoever shall not be offended in me."

These were the wonderful works by which Jesus was proved, according to Nicodemus's statement, to have come from God; and I myself think they are full proof of the God power. I submit, that if the logic of Jesus was good, and he presented this as a proof of the divinity of his mission, it would prove as much for any other person doing the same work. I myself have seen mediums do all that Jesus claims to have done, with the exception of raising the dead; and I have known of that being done in the same sense that Jesus did it. No Jesus, nor any other person, ever raised an absolutely dead person to life. As well talk of organizing a dozen bacon hams into the form of a human body, and making them live. Persons have gone into a cataleptic state, and been supposed to be dead, and have been reanimated. It not unfrequently occurs that doctors pronounce persons dead who are not dead. Certificates of burial are granted for persons who outlived those who signed them. The writer of this volume was once measured for a coffin; he also has a brother who has been pronounced dead at four different periods of his life. Should any one undertake to bury him now, after being four times scientifically dead, they would find a hard corpse to handle.

The maid that orthodoxy accuses Jesus of raising from the dead, had not been dead. At least, Jesus said of her, "She is not dead, but sleepeth." (Luke viii. 51.) Of Lazarus, Jesus said, "This sickness is not unto death, but for the glory of God." (John xi. 4.) Lazarus was supposed to be dead and entombed, it is true, so was a lady in Quincy, Ill., but she astonished the multitude by coming out of the tomb. The daily papers report that a lady was sent from Chicago, Ill., to Rochester, N. Y., for burial, but when she got there was resuscitated, and returned to her home. J. H. Weaver, an undertaker in Baltimore, Md., informed me that in removing dead bodies he had found several that had evidently come to life and struggled to get out of their coffins.

I have to-day clipped the following from the Cincinnati Commercial of February 20, 1872: —

"The Oshkosh Times says, Mr. Fuss, proprietor of the Fuss House, at Menasha, Wisconsin, was thought to have died on the 8th inst., and preparations were made for the burial. The funeral was postponed until the 11th, when the friends of the deceased gathered to the last rites. Just before the coffin was closed some of the friends noticed that the supposed corpse was perspiring quite freely. A physician was called in, who proceeded to bleed the man, when the blood flowed, and he soon came too and recognized the anxious mourners. He is now doing well, and in a fair way of recovery."

The following is from the Cincinnati Gazette of March 5, 1872:—

"A man was found at Hall's Corners, Westchester County, N. Y., on Monday night, apparently frozen to death. The body was taken to Tarrytown, and the coroner from Hastings held an inquest over it, a verdict being rendered accordingly. The body was placed in a coffin, and started for Sleepy Hollow Cemetery. As the coffin was about to be lowered into the grave, a noise proceeded from it, causing the interment to be delayed long enough to discover that the man was alive. Last night the supposed corpse was sitting by the fire at the Farrington Depot, reflecting on things earthly. His name has not been ascertained."

Professor S. B. Britton, on page 471–2 of " Man and his Relations " (a work that every thinker should study), relates the history of the burial and resurrection of a man who was, by artificial means, thrown into a cataleptic state. The man, after being buried *ten months*, and having a crop of barley raised on his grave, was restored to life. This case is well authenticated; so are numerous others. I submit that they border as much on the miraculous as any recorded in the Bible. Permit me to give the history of two cases, as great, at least, as the resurrection of Lazarus.

Mr. Britton says, " Some time since the writer received from E. G. Fuller, Esq., a gentleman of unquestioned intelligence and veracity, — whose residence is in Cold Water, Mich., — the main facts of a case of peculiar interest, and which will afford a striking illustration of my subject. Columbia Lancaster, a lawyer, who formerly lived in Centreville, St. Joseph's County, Mich., removed, in the autumn of 1840, to Missouri, with a view to going to Oregon, in the spring of 1841. He accordingly started, and pursued his course to the distance of several days' journey beyond Fort Laramie, when his wife, who accompanied him, became seriously ill. He waited a day or two, in the hope that Mrs. L. would speedily recover. But her illness continued, and he directed the rest of the company — except one man who remained to assist him in the care of his wife — to proceed on their way, himself designing to follow them as soon as the patient was sufficiently recovered, or to return should she be unable to continue the journey.

" But Mrs. Lancaster grew worse, and the man who remained with Mr. Lancaster and his lady, was sent back to Fort Laramie for medicines. He had been gone but a short time when the patient expired. Mr. Lancaster remained there with the form of his fair companion, until the man came back from the Fort. On his return he was accompanied by two Indians, who were strongly attached to Mrs. Lancaster, on account of her previous kindness to them. The Indians formed a litter, by placing blankets and other suitable articles on poles. On this rude carriage the body was placed, and the Indians conveyed it some three hundred miles through the wilderness, fording streams, and surmounting whatever obstacles were in the way. On arriving at Fort Laramie, preparations were made for the funeral; but before the remains were finally disposed of, and *eight days after Mrs. Lancaster was supposed to have died, the body exhibited signs of returning life, and by degrees was fully restored!* When Mrs. Lancaster had so far recovered as to be able to converse, she assured her friends that she was all the while perfectly conscious of everything that occurred, and she even related the conversation and several incidents that transpired during the journey."

The same author, on pages 479 and 480, has the following: "The case of Rev. William Tennent, of New Jersey, a clergyman of the Presbyterian branch of the church, is one of the most remarkable on record. While conversing with his brother in Latin respecting the state of the soul, and his prospects in the life to come, he expressed doubts concerning his future happiness. Just at that moment he suddenly lost the power of speech and voluntary motion: he was apparently insensible, and his friends believed that the spirit had vacated its earthly tabernacle. Arrangements were accordingly made for the appropriate solemnities; but his physician, who was also a warm personal friend, was not satisfied, and at his request the funeral rites were delayed. Three days passed; the eyes were rayless, the lips discolored, and the body cold and stiff. The brother insisted that the remains should be entombed. The critical hour at length arrived, the people had assembled, and the occasion was about to be solemnized by appropriate ceremonies, when the whole company were startled by a fearful groan! The eyes were opened for a moment but closed again, and the form remained silent and motionless for an hour. Again a heavy groan proceeded from the body, and the eyes were opened; but in an instant all signs of returning animation had vanished.

"After another interval of an hour, life and consciousness, with the power of voluntary motion, were measurably restored. After his restoration, it was found that Mr. Tennent had lost all recollection of his former life, and the results of his education and experience were wholly obliterated from his mind. He was obliged to learn the alphabet of his vernacular. His memory at length returned, and with it his former mental possessions; but his doubts respecting a future life were all dissipated for ever. During his absence from the body he was intromitted to the heavens, and, like Paul, heard and saw things unutterable. The trances and visions of the ancient prophets and apostles were intrinsically no more remarkable than this experience of Mr. Tennent."

While on this subject, it may not be amiss to add that Victoria C. Woodhull relates, and actually believes, that her son was dead, and she, by her mediumistic power, restored him to life.

It is true that mediums do not always succeed in their undertakings: neither did Jesus. When they were offended at Jesus in his own country, where he was the *best* known, and his power the *best* understood, he answered, "A prophet is not without honor, save in his own country, and his own house." The evangelist adds, "And he did not many mighty works there, because of their unbelief." (Matt. xiii. 58.)

A case that at once illustrates Jesus' power, and lack of power, is found in John v. 1–9. "After this there was a feast of the Jews, and Jesus went up to Jerusalem. Now there is at Jerusalem by the sheep market a pool, which is called in the Hebrew tongue Bethesda, having five porches. In these lay a great multitude of impotent folk, of blind, halt, withered, waiting for the moving of the water. For an angel went down at a certain season into the pool, and troubled the water: whosoever then first after the troubling of the water stepped in was made whole of whatsoever disease he had. And a certain man was there, which had an infirmity thirty and eight years. When Jesus saw him lie, and knew that he had been now a long time in that case, he saith unto him, Wilt thou be made whole? The impotent man answered him, Sir, I have no man, when the water is troubled, to put me into the pool: but while I am coming another steppeth down before me. Jesus saith unto him, Rise, take up thy bed and walk. And immediately the man was made whole, and took up his bed and walked; and on the same day was the Sabbath."

No statement could be more clear than this. Here was a pool, where an angel went down at a certain season and troubled the water; then *the first* one who stepped into the pool after the water was troubled, was made whole. Thus it appears that one was healed every year; but as the sick rushed there by hundreds to be healed, and only one could be healed, at the annual troubling of the waters, the multitudes of sick and impotent folks increased until, John says, there was a *great multitude*. Jesus, in looking over this "great multitude," found one, only one, of the great number that his clairvoyant perceptions told him he could heal, and, after the conversation above related, healed the one, and left all the rest to die there, or be healed at the slow rate of one, "at a certain season." This multitude increasing every day, rendered the chances of being healed at the pool hardly worth staying for.

I have, in my own experience as a healer, met parallel cases. Probably one case in a hundred of sick people that I see impresses me with an almost irresistible impulse to heal them, and in such cases I seldom fail. On the other hand, any medium will occasionally get the opposite feeling. In such cases, all the efforts of that medium will prove ineffectual. This was probably the case with Jesus, and will account for his healing one case, and going away and leaving so many sick folks at the pool of Siloam.

The day of Pentecost is by Christians referred to with great confidence as being especially prolific of evidences of the divinity of Christianity; and I must confess I know of no chapter in the Bible better calculated to portray the benefit arising from phenomenal Christianity. The works done on the day of Pentecost can be enumerated as follows: —

1. The falling upon the disciples or mediums of a spiritual influence, called the Holy Ghost.

2. The speaking of different languages by the aid of spirit power.

3. Peter preaching under spirit influence; and,

4. Soon after the Pentecost, and during the revival that then commenced, the healing of a cripple.

No one claims that any other evidence of the divinity of the Christian system than the four points mentioned can be drawn out of this revival. Now, can ten thousand witnesses be believed, when they declare, upon their sacred honor, that they have, at different times, witnessed all of these phenomena in modern Spiritualism. Do these things prove the divinity of Christianity? If so, permit them to do as much for that which now produces them. But I must argue more than is embraced in the proposition that the arguments used, in defense of Christianity apply with all their force to modern Spiritualism. Let me state, as a second proposition, that

EVERY ARGUMENT URGED AGAINST SPIRITUALISM APPLIES WITH ALL ITS FORCE AGAINST THE BIBLE.

I shall not now thoroughly argue every point that could be discussed under the above heading, as many of the points must come up in other divisions of this book. The reply to the oft-repeated arguments on the immoralities of Spiritualism, will be made in a chapter devoted to the comparative moral tendencies of the two systems.

It is sometimes said that Spiritualism has in it a great deal that is ridiculous and silly. I do not know but this is true: I am inclined to think there are some incongruities and absurdities in it. There are fools in this world, and there may be in the other. I notice fools sometimes pass over the river of death. Solomon says, "Though thou shouldest bray a fool in the mortar among wheat, with a pestle, yet will not his foolishness depart from him." I presume that even the mortar and pestle of death have failed to pulverize the folly of some who have passed through that ordeal.

But is there nothing silly or absurd in the Bible? Is there anything in Spiritualism more silly than the angel's *tête-à-tête* with Moses at the country tavern when he tried to kill him? (Ex. iv. 24, 25.) Did the reader ever notice the tedious and silly way that Gideon took to talk with his God? (Judges vi. 36–40.) What could be more silly than the manner in which God told Gideon to test his army? (Judges vii. 4.) If a spirit were to say, "I will hiss for the fly of Egypt," or, "I will shave with a razor that is hired"? (See Isa. vii. 18, 20), would not the opposers find in that all the evidence they could wish that Spiritualism was disgustingly silly? Yet, when the Bible represents God as doing these things, I would be called sacrilegious if I were to deny them. Were a medium to record that a spirit wrestled with him all night, and finally threw him down and broke his thigh, he would be laughed at by every Christian in the land. But let one dare to make sport of the wrestling-match between God and Jacob, and he does it at the risk of religious and social ostracism. (See Gen. xxiv. 30.)

There are not so many now as in former times who deny spirit manifestations. The age for that is about past. If it were not, I would ask by what rule the wonderful stories in the Bible can be believed, and stories now just like them, only not half so large, established by ten times the amount of testimony, must be rejected? To illustrate: Christians find no trouble in believing that Jesus came to the disciples after his *anastasis* and ate fish and honeycomb; but when I tell the same persons, who find it no stretch of their credulity to believe this story, that I can prove by a hundred good witnesses, some of them not Spiritualists, that spirits came into Mrs. Kegwin's circles in Jeffersonville, Ind., and ate apples in the presence of the whole circle, they are ready to swear that I and my witnesses are imposing on their credulity. Now, though this statement is true, I do not ask Bible believers to receive it; I only ask them to be consistent, and reject the story of the spirits eating the calf, and Jesus eating after his death. (See Gen. xviii. 8; Luke xxiv. 30, 43, 44; Acts x. 41.)

The objection that Spiritualism comes from the devil, was made with equal vehemence and truthfulness against John and Jesus. (Matt. xi. 18; xii. 24; John vii. 20; viii. 48.)

The objection against darkness being one of the conditions for certain of the manifestations of spirit power, would weigh against many portions of the Bible. That book declares that "God dwells in the midst of thick darkness." (1 Kings viii. 12.) God's wrestle with Jacob was in the dark. As soon as it began to get light God could do nothing more — could not even get away from Jacob, and began to devoutly pray for Jacob to let him go, "for the day breaketh." (Gen. xxxii. 24.) The pulling of the linchpins out of Pharaoh's chariot-wheels was done in the dark. So the resurrection of Jesus was a work of darkness. It was night when the walls of Jericho fell, and in fact almost every biblical wonder transpired in the dark.

I will now offer another proposition, viz. : —

THE EVIDENCES OF THE TRUTH OF THE BIBLE ARE NOT SO CONCLUSIVE AS THOSE OF MODERN SPIRITUALISM.

No one will dispute that the evidences of the authenticity, genuineness, and integrity of the Bible is second-hand evidence. If ever there was first-class evidence of the teachings, it has not reached us. But even if this was not true, if we had the privilege of consulting the original witnesses, they were not such witnesses as would now be taken as the best evidence of such manifestations as they record. The people among whom the prophets, Jesus, and the apostles did their wonders, were not educated as the multitudes now are. Not one in one thousand of them could read, much less had they a scientific education. Many of the now very simple phenomena were to them entirely unexplainable, and hence miraculous. The prophets, Jesus, and the apostles never had the good fortune to have to do any wonders among any people that were in advance of the Cheyennes or Camanches of to-day. When they became civilized enough to want to build a perpetual residence for their God (1 Kings viii. 12, 13), they were compelled to send to a heathen king for skilled workmen. They had not one among all their workmen capable of doing the work. (1 Kings v. 6.)

Now think of the biblical wonders being wrought among these ignoramuses, then think of the stories passing from mouth to mouth, and the verbal inaccuracies necessarily attending such stories, and that they are only preserved by these hearsay reports, and I think all will see the necessity of making calculations for their growth. Now, reader, please add to the above considerations the fact that there were no Argus-eyed reporters on the spot to criticise and ridicule the manifestations; no interviewers to interview either the miracle-workers or those who beheld them, and the chances for deception become so great and numerous that the stories must be received with allowance.

No one, I think, will fail to recognize that while the above is true of all the Bible wonders, it is not true of modern spirit manifestations. They are wrought among the *literati* of the age. Many of them are recorded on the spot by eye-witnesses; reporters and interviewers are frequently on the *arena;* every mistake is recorded and heralded by the daily press. Rigid scientific and theologic tests are applied, and every precaution to prevent deception. Those witnessing the phenomena are brought into court, and compelled to tell their stories under the pains and penalties of perjury. Thus the truth, the whole truth, and nothing but the truth, is elicited in the presence of those who have witnesses on the ground, and have laid every snare to entrap the witness of these wonders. Astute lawyers are well paid for exhausting their skill in examining and cross-examining witnesses, all to no purpose, save to deepen the general conviction that the manifestations said to have a spiritual origin do occur.

But should I withdraw the foregoing argument, and admit that the witnesses of the manifestations occurring in the presence of Jesus and the apostles were in every instance good, educated, honorable witnesses, still your testimony for biblical manifestations is not so good as ours for those occurring in the present century. Biblical testimonies have been translated too often, and passed through too many hands. No one can know now whether it was true or not. Aside from the corroboration of modern facts, the evidences that they ever occurred have passed through entirely too many hands, and been tinkered too often. It would be impossible now to know their truth.

On this subject Lardner, the great Christian author, in his Cred. Gos. Hist., vol. iv. p. 524, quotes Casaubon, as follows:—

"It mightily affects me to see how many there are in the earliest times of the church who considered it a capital exploit to lend heavenly truth the help of their inventions, in order that the new doctrines might be more readily allowed by the wise among the Gentiles. These officious lies, they were wont to say, were devised for a good end."

Hundreds of other Christian authors have freely spoken on the same subject. Selmer shows the chances for deception with regard to facts in the case. He says,—

"The Christian doctors never brought their sacred books before the common people, although people in general have been wont to think otherwise. During the first ages they were in the hands of the clergy only."

The tendency of good Christian people to lie for the glory of God, and sometimes manufacture whole stories, may be learned from the following from Bishop Heliodorus: "A falsehood is a good thing when it aids the speaker and does no injury to the hearers."

Other Christian writers strengthen our faith in the

records they have handed us, in the following manner: —

Bishop Marsh says, "It is a certain fact, that several readings of our common printed text are mere alterations made by Origen, whose authority was so great in the Christian church, that emendations which he proposed, though, as he himself acknowledged, they were supported by the evidence of no manuscript, were very generally received." And Origen himself, speaking of the gospels, says, "There are things contained therein, which, taken in their literal sense, are mere falsities and lies." — *Hom.* 6, *in Isaiah,* fol. 107, D.

Origen admits, says Du Pin, that "there is a great discrepancy between the copies, which must be attributed either to the negligence of the scribes, or to the audacious perversions of others, or to those who correct the text by arbitrary additions or omissions, who oftentimes have put in and left out as they thought it most convenient."

Gregory Nazianzen says, " A little jargon is all that is necessary to impose on the people. The less they comprehend, the more they admire!"

Not only has the Bible and its history passed through a great many hands, and thus been subject to the mistakes of transcribers and translators, but it has been in *bad* hands.

The following testimonies from eminent Christians will let the reader somewhat into the light as to how far those who have handed us the stories we are expected to believe can be trusted: —

Ignatius (A. D. 107) says, "Now the virginity of Mary, and he who was born of her, was kept in secret from the prince of this world, as was also the death of our Lord; three of the mysteries most spoken of throughout the world, yet done in secret by God."

If this historical fact, stated by an apostolic father, can be believed, it is doubtful whether Mary was a virgin, or any of the miracles of Jesus were ever wrought.

Bishop Horseley states that Origen "was not incapable of asserting in argument what he believed not, and that a strict regard to truth in disputation was not one of the virtues of his character." . . . "Time was when the practice of using unjustifiable means to serve a good cause was openly avowed, and Origen himself was among its defenders."

Eusebius heads the thirty-first chapter of his Evangelical Preparation, with the following query: —

"How far may it be proper to use falsehood as a medicine, and for the benefit of those who require to be deceived." In another place he takes occasion to laud himself thus: "I have related whatever might redound to the glory, and I have suppressed all that could tend to the disgrace, of our religion."

Mosheim (vol. i. p. 120) says, "The authors who have treated of the innocence and sanctity of the primitive Christians, have fallen into the error of supposing them to have been unspotted models of piety and virtue, and a gross error indeed it is, as the strongest testimonies too evidently prove."

On p. 198, vol. i., he says, "In the fourth century it was an almost universally adopted maxim, that it was an act of virtue to deceive and lie, when, by such means, the interests of the church might be promoted."

Dr. Whitby says, Papias and Iræneus have "handed down the actions of the apostles and their disciples from paltry rumors and dubious reports, and as having scandalously deluded the world with fables and lying narrations." — *De Script. Interpreted*, p. 73.

St. Hermas exclaims, "O Lord, I never spake a true word in my life; but I have always lived in dissimulation, and affirmed a lie for truth to all men, and no man contradicted me."

Daille, on the use of the fathers, says, "Neither ought we to wonder that even those of the honest, innocent, primitive times made use of those deceits, saying for a good end they made no scruples of forging whole books."

He quotes Celsus as saying, "They altered the Gospels three or four different times, as if they were drunk, and when pressed by their adversaries, recurred to that reading which best suited their purpose!"

St. Jerome says, "I do not find fault with an error which proceeds from hatred towards the Jews, and a pious zeal for the Christian faith." — *Oper.*, tom. 4, p. 113.

Michaelis, in the Preface to his Translations, says, "No one will deny that the early Christians who differed from the ruling church, have altered the New Testament in numerous examples, according to their peculiar tenets." "And, so much so," says the Rev. Mr. Nolan, in his Inquiry, p. 460, "that little confidence could be placed in any edition."

Du Pin says, "It cannot be said that no fault has crept into the Scriptures by the negligence or inadvertency of the transcribers, or even by the boldness of those who have ventured to strike out, add, or change some words which they thought necessary to be omitted, added, or changed."

St. Synesius says, "The people are desirous of being deceived. We can not act otherwise respecting them."

With all this array of testimony as to the character of the fathers in the church, — those to whom we are indebted for the Bible and all its contents, — who can do otherwise than doubt whether the big stories in the book may not have been put in there by those who esteemed it "a virtue to lie and deceive, when by it the cause of the church can be advanced."

THE INTERNAL EVIDENCES OF THE BIBLE NOT GOOD.

If appeal be made from the departments of the subjects already presented to the internal testimonies of the truth of the Bible and the divinity of its teachings, I must answer, Your witness testifies against you. The subject of the purity of biblical teachings, as compared with Spiritualism, will come up in another chapter. Now I only inquire after the historical truth of some of its statements.

Gen. xiv. 14, says, "And when Abram heard that his brother was taken captive, he armed his trained servants, born in his own house, three hundred and eighteen, and pursued them unto Dan." Does any one believe this? What would you think of the historian who would tell you that Alexander the Great pursued his enemies even unto Washington? Would you not call that an anachronism? The truth is, the city of Dan had no existence for more than four centuries after Abraham was "asleep with his fathers."

In Judges xviii. 28, 29, the historian records, that, "They [the children of Dan] built a city and dwelt therein. And they called the name of the city Dan, after the name of Dan, their father, who was born unto Israel; howbeit, the name of the city was Laish at the first." Dan was the great grandson of Abraham; it was Dan's great-great grandchildren that built the city and named it after him. Will the one who thinks the Bible all true and Spiritualism all false, tell us how Abraham chased his enemies to Dan so long before the great grandfather of those who built it was born?

The contradictory stories concerning Ahaziah's age, one recorded in 2 Kings viii. 6, the other in 2 Chron. xxii. 2, can not both be correct. It is not probable that either of them is true. They both make Ahaziah the youngest son of Jehoram. The statement in the Book of Kings would make Ahaziah only eighteen years younger than his father, which was not at all probable. The Book of Chronicles makes him two years older than his father, which was impossible.

As an instance of the unreliability of portions of the book which we are asked to credit rather than modern Spiritualism, I will refer the reader to the quail story, found in Num. xi. 31: "And there went forth a wind from the Lord, and brought quails from the sea, and let them fall by the camp, as it were a day's journey on this side, and as it were a day's journey on the other side, round about the camp, and as it were two cubits high upon the face of the earth."

According to this story the pile of quails must have been forty-four inches high and sixty-six miles in diameter. The story is too large. The story of

Samson slaying a thousand men with a jawbone of an ass, is too large. (See Judges xv. 15.) Men do not voluntarily walk up to be slaughtered in that way. Should they become insane enough to do so, the weapon Samson used is not sufficient. The second part of the story about the jawbone becoming the source of a stream of water is worse than the first,—it beats Jack the Giant-Killer, or Sindbad the Sailor. I really wish Samson had picked up the jawbone and thrown it into the stream that ran out of the hollow place in it. He might have imparted information as to whether it would sink or swim!

The story of Samson and his three hundred foxes with burning tails destroying thousands of acres of green corn (Judges, xv. 3, 5), represents Samson as being a more than ordinarily good fox-hunter, so much so that now it is generally considered a fit companion of Gulliver's Travels.

Without referring the reader to other portions of the Old and New Testaments, proving the unreliability of their contents, I submit another proposition, viz.: —

A DESTRUCTION OF THE EVIDENCES OF SPIRITUALISM WOULD DESTROY THE BIBLE.

In another proposition I argued that any argument used against modern Spiritualism would weigh with all its force against the Bible; but in this proposition I mean more than I did in that.

Can the dead, or can they not, return? If I am answered that they can return, then the foundation of modern Spiritualism is admitted. If they can not return, then the Bible is not true, for it says Samuel did come back and talk to Saul. (1 Sam. xxviii. 21.) Elijah did give a communication to the king Jehoram, and that in his own handwriting. (2 Chron. xxi. 12.) He did come back, using John the Baptist as a medium. (Luke i. 17.) Moses and Elias did come to Jesus on the mount of transfiguration (Matt. xvii. 1-9), and seven spirits, one of them John's own brother, came to him on the Island of Patmos. (Rev. xxi. 10-12; ii. 8.)

I now ask, Are these things true? If they are, Spiritualism is true; if not, the Bible is false. Take the case of Samuel to illustrate the argument. Did he come back? If so, he has proved there is a means of communication between the two worlds; since, if there had not been, he could not have come back. If, on the other hand, he did not come back, then the Bible, which says he did, relates a falsehood, and its veracity is destroyed by its indorsement of Spiritualism.

Once more I ask, Will you believe me, and dozens of other witnesses, when we say we have seen spirit hands formed, and take a pencil and write on a slate, — often in exactly the hand they wrote when in earth life? If not, how can you believe the Bible when it says, "In the same hour came forth fingers of a man's hand, and wrote over against the candlestick upon the plaster of the wall of the king's palace: and the king saw the part of the hand that wrote. Then the king's countenance was changed, and his thoughts troubled him, so that the joints of his loins were loosed, and his knees smote one against another." (Dan. v. 5, 6.)

LIVING WITNESSES.

One great advantage Spiritualism has over the marvellous stories related in the Bible is, that Spiritualists are not compelled to look through the musty histories of many hundreds of years standing for evidence of its truth. Provided that the spiritual stories and Bible stories were all the same, it must be conceded that the great balance of testimony is in favor of Spiritualism. In the case of Spiritualism, the witnesses are alive, and in the vicinity of every reader of this volume. There is not one who reads this book who could not, in twenty-four hours' time, get the sworn testimony of witnesses enough to prove any point that can be proved by testimony. He can cross-examine the witnesses, and look into the chances for deception, *ad libitum*. Not so with biblical wonders: they may, or they may not, have occurred. There are no witnesses to-day of the resurrection of Lazarus; no opportunity is offered to detect fraud and trickery. Nothing is known of the names, much less of the moral character or intellectual attainments, of those who testified in this case, if, indeed, there were any to bear testimony. One case will fully illustrate my meaning. It is said that the walls of Jericho fell down when the children of Israel marched around them. Now imagine how a conversation would run between a Spiritualist and a Christian on the subject. Let the Spiritualist commence by asking the question, Do you believe the story of the falling of the walls of Jericho at the time of the great march of the children of Israel around them?

Christian. Certainly I do; it is in the Bible; why should I not believe it?

Spir. Knowing that Christians are some of them very doubtful of wonderful manifestations, when backed by what seems to me very conclusive evidence, I did not know but that you even doubted this story. Since you inform me that you believe the record of this wonderful manifestation, will you be kind enough to tell me why you believe it?

Chris. Because it is in the Bible; what more is needed?

Spir. When did this wonderful story find its way into the Bible?

Chris. I do not know.

Spir. What was the moral and intellectual character of the writer?

Chris. I can't say; I guess it must have been good.

Spir. Who was he? What was his name?

Chris. I do not know as the name of the author is given. In fact, I know that scholars do not *pretend* to know who wrote the narrative.

Spir. Do you know of any corroborative history in the world?

Chris. Not any.

Spir. Then why do you believe the story?

Chris. Because it is in the Bible.

Spir. I will tell you why I think it possible the story may be true. I have seen tables shaken and moved by spirit power alone, when no visible power touched them. Spirits that can shake tables may have shaken prison doors open, or the walls of Jericho down.

Chris. Don't talk to me about spirits shaking tables. I can't believe such big stories.

EVIDENCE OF THE BIBLE AND SPIRITUALISM. 63

Thus you see, dear reader, what a strange admixture there must be in that organism which believes all the Bible and yet rejects modern Spiritualism, established by ten thousand times the amount of evidence.

Consistency is a rare jewel; let us always try to keep a good stock of it on hand.

"What is the Past, with its psalms and prayers?
   And what are its crude beliefs to me?
Men never *saw*, in the Present of theirs,
   What is denied for the *Now* to see!
The years that are gone are as stranger men
We passed, but shall never pass again.

"Mine is the Present, *now, this hour;*
   Shall I be the dupe of a dupe of yore?
And see a revealment of heavenly power
   In the rag of a gaberdine he wore?
The rag of a web spun long ago,
Might have covered a fool, for aught I know.

"And John may have dreamed, away down East,
   In the Isle of Patmos — God knows where; —
But what to me is his horned beast,
   His thrones, and his mammoth angel there?
The dream of John to my spirit means
Nothing more strange than another's dreams.

"And Christ may have suffered upon the tree,
   And died for the sins of those who stood
To see him die. But he's naught more to me
   Than are *other* men who suffered for good.
Their blood — as his — by the hand of power
Was shed for the faith of the living hour."

CHAPTER III.

TEACHINGS OF THE BIBLE AND SPIRITUALISM.

The Boast of Christians. — Age of the Bible no Argument in its favor. — A few knotty Questions. — Author does not dispute the Designs of Christianity. — Testimonies of Christians on the failure of Christianity. — Christians accuse each other. — Paul in a Dilemma. — His Plan of Escape. — Confessions of modern Christians. — Jesus' Parables leading in the wrong Direction. — The prodigal Son. — The unjust Steward. — Jesus commends the Scoundrel. — The unjust Judge. — Reasons for prayer. — The Laborers in the Vineyard. — Does God play the same Game. — Bad Precepts. — Borrowing of the Egyptians. — Children of Israel not Slaves in Egypt. — What to do with bad Meat. — Punishment for religious Differences. — Treatment of bad Boys. — The Bible on Slavery. — On the treatment of Slaves. — The war upon the Midianites. — Biblical Temperance. — Sketches from Jesus' Sermon. — Jesus a disturber of domestic Relations. — A cool Reception. — Immoral Doctrines. — Works of no avail. — Character of the biblical God. — The Difference. — The *modus operandi* of Salvation. — Proper Generation *vs.* Regeneration. — Recipe for making Hogs of Children. — How to cure Depravity. — Rest when Nature rests; work when she works. — North and South ends of People. — Ten syllogistic Arguments. — Conclusion.

By the time the argument on Spiritualism and the Bible has reached the crisis to which the last chapter brought it, the advocates of the Bible as opposed to Spiritualism begin to get their fears terribly aroused, least Spiritualism should lead people away from the high moral, mental, and spiritual bearing to which the teachings and practice of those who made, and those who now regard the Bible as the " Book of books," has elevated them. The boast of the Christian world is, that in the Bible as a book, and in the history of the characters who vouchsafed it to us, we have the highest possible type of moral, mental, and spiritual purity. The Bible is nothing else than God's own book, and therefore perfect. The moral lessons taught in it are so perfect that by no possibility could they be improved, and the character of its heroes, commonly called saints, are worthy to be held up as an example for all coming generations. In this connection of eulogizing the Bible and its Moguls, its advocates generally say, " There is no kind of use in attacking the Bible now, it has stood too long. Marcion, Porphyry, and Julian made an attack on it; Gibbon, Hume, Voltaire, and Paine undertook to put it down, but after nineteen hundred years of warfare it stands yet, a monument of strength against which it is foolish to battle."

This is in part true. Christianity stands to-day, but I am led to ask, *cui bono?* The Christian has one argument in favor of his system, that is, its age. Catholicism is old: is it therefore divine? How about Mohammedanism? Paganism is older yet than Christianity, and still it stands against the attacks of Christian missionaries; let us argue its divinity from its age. Sin is older than any religion; religions have tried in vain to crush it out, still it stands an impregnable bulwark. Shall we therefore plead with Christianity to cease its warfare upon sin?

Now that I have been frank enough to admit the fact that Christianity is old, how will the advocates of the system make that an argument in its favor? The question is not one of age, but what has it done for the world? How has the world been benefited by tolerating the institution so long? Has it made the world better? Has it redeemed humanity? Has it caused its own adherents to beat their swords into ploughshares and their spears into pruning-hooks, and do they learn war no more? Are the lives of even those who profess to enjoy the blessings of Christianity, who practice its virtues, models of perfection and purity? Are Christians to-day, or have they ever been, governed by the golden rule, any more than those whom it denominates infidels? Nay, do not Christians themselves confess that the world has steadily increased in wickedness under its administration? Whether true or not, evangelical ministers, books, and papers to-day tell the people there never was so much wickedness in the world as at the present time. How is it that sin increases in proportion as a knowledge of Christianity and its Bible abounds? By and by I shall have a few words in answer to this question. I now suggest that nearly nineteen hundred years of failure is enough to show that there is something radically wrong in the system. I am led to think that if Christianity is to save the world at all, it is time it was about it. Let us have a change of physicians.

I have not the slightest doubt of the desire on the part of many good Christians to benefit the world, but good desires are not enough. With all their desires, their love of approbation, and the pride of their system, Christians have not even been able to keep themselves morally pure. Let us, writer and readers, now, not as theorizers or fault-finders, but as honest men in search of the truth, see why Christianity has failed, and see whether there is anything else that will do what it has failed to accomplish. That Christians themselves regard that their system has thus far failed in its work is evident. The following extracts are all from Christian authorities: —

Elder M. E. Cornell says, "It is not with any desire to find fault, or, like the wordling, to dwell upon the imperfections of others, and make their backslidings an excuse for laxity, that we speak of the fallen condition of the churches, for we do it with sadness, and would God it were otherwise. The facts are so well known to keen-eyed skeptics, infidels, and the world at large, that if we refuse to acknowledge them it would indicate a want of honesty on our part. But while infidels rejoice over the matter, and make it an occasion of doubting and rejecting the Bible and the Christian religion, we note the facts with candor, and see in it a fulfillment of prophecy. Instead of an occasion of stumbling, we find it an occasion of stronger faith in the Bible, as of heavenly origin. But while we speak freely on the subject, we need not appear before the world as confessing for the churches, as though they were unwilling to acknowledge the facts; for this they have fully done for themselves, as will appear from the copious extracts in the following pages. Let not the unbeliever rejoice over the fallen state of the church, for it is an omen of no good to the world. If the truth has lost its power upon its professed friends, what can its enemies hope for?"

Alexander Campbell says, "The worshiping establishments now in operation throughout Christendom, increased and cemented by their respective voluminous confessions of faith, and their ecclesiastical constitutions, are not churches of Jesus Christ, but the legitimate daughters of that mother of harlots, the Church of Rome."

Lorenzo Dow says of the Romish Church, "If she be a *mother*, who are the *daughters?* It must be the corrupt, national, established churches that came out of her." — *Dow's Life*, p. 542.

In the Religious Encyclopedia (art. Antichrist), we read, " The writer of the Book of Revelation tells us he heard a voice from heaven, saying, ' Come out of her, my people, that ye partake not of her sins, and receive not of her plagues.' If such persons are to be found in the ' mother of harlots,' with much less hesitation may it be inferred that they are connected with her unchaste daughters, those national churches which are founded upon what are called *Protestant principles*."

Robert Atkins, in a sermon preached in London, says, " The truly righteous are diminished from the earth, and no man layeth it to heart. The professors of religion of the present day in every church are lovers of the world, conformers to the world, lovers of creature-comfort, and aspirers after respectability. They are called to suffer with Christ, but they shrink from even reproach. Apostasy, apostasy, apostasy, is engraven on the very front of every church; and did they know it, and did they feel it, there might be hope ; but, alas! they cry, 'We are rich, and increased in goods, and stand in need of nothing.' "

The report of the Michigan Yearly Conference, published in the True Wesleyan of November 15, 1851, says, " The world, commercial, political, and ecclesiastical, are alike, and are together going in the broad way that leads to death. Politics, commerce, and nominal religion, all connive at sin, reciprocally aid each other, and unite to crush the poor. Falsehood is unblushingly uttered in the forum and in the pulpit, and sins that would shock the moral sensibilities of the heathen go unrebuked in all the great denominations of our land." These churches are like the Jewish church when the Saviour exclaimed, "Wo unto you, scribes and Pharisees, hypocrites."

Henry Ward Beecher says, "All the framework of society seems to be dissolving. On every side we find men false to the most important trusts. Even the judges on the bench are bought and sold like meat in the shambles. One must go into court with a long purse to obtain justice. The judiciary of New York stinks like Sodom and Gomorrah. Men say they hardly know a court in which to trust a case. It is no longer an honor to sit on the bench, for if the judge be an upright man his character will be contaminated by the great majority of his associates."

Says the New York Tribune, "The telegraph wires bend under their weight of woe; the old earth quivers with throbs of agony from the center to the pole; cities are shaken down, countries are ingulfed, fair domains are overflowed with red-hot lava; wife is arrayed against husband, mother against child, son against father; a hecatomb is sacrificed on one railway, half as many on another, and on still another the width of a hair stands between a thousand and sudden death. In social life, our newspapers are smutched all over with reports of divorce and separation trials, of infidelity and disgrace, of gigantic crimes undertaken, half accomplished, or completed. What shall be the end of these things?"

The Christian Inquirer says, "Such an intense and insane rush and struggle for wealth, such reckless, ruinous, extravagance of expenditure, such a delirium for vulgar display, this country has never seen.

And, alas! not only taste, refinement, purity, and piety have gone down before the tide, but even honesty, &c. . . . Every vice has increased in an alarming degree. Intemperance — not only are our streets and public places full of it, not only do young men and old men and mere boys fall before it by scores and hundreds, but even women, beautiful, accomplished, beloved wives and daughters carry its fire-blush on their cheeks, and reel and totter under its influence on the sidewalks. There are more gaming places in the city to-day than there were dry goods stores twenty years ago; and the gamblers include all classes, from the boy of fifteen to the *roue* of fifty. But why enumerate? Every vice on the black catalogue of transgression has more than doubled in volume and in victims within these five years, and our youth, the pride and hope of our land, are falling beneath the subtle destroyer faster than ever they fell in Southern campaign."

A writer in the New York Tribune, speaking of the fashionable religion and worship of this boasted age of progress, says, "Now the worshipers one after another glide in, silks rattle, plumes wave, satins glisten, diamonds glitter, and scores of forty-dollar handkerchiefs shake out their perfumed odors! What absurdity to preach the gospel of the lowly Nazarite to such a set! The clergyman knows better than to do so. He values his fat salary and handsome parsonage too highly. So with a velvety tread he walks all around the ten commandments — places the downiest pillow under the dying profligate's head, and ushers him with seraphic hymning into an upper-ten Heaven."

A Christian poet, in a long lamentation on the departure of piety and religion from the church, says, —

> "Her pastors love to live at ease;
> They covet wealth and honor;
> And while they seek such things as these,
> They bring reproach upon her.
> Such worthless objects they pursue,
> Warmly and undiverted,
> The church they lead and ruin, too —
> Her glory is departed.

From these extracts, and hundreds of similar ones which I have at command, the reader can not help but see that Christians themselves have written their system down a failure. Like the ancient prophets, who had no confidence in each other's predictions, they spend their time in accusing each other, as we have noted in the foregoing extracts. Those who have been accustomed to attend love-feasts, conferences, or even to hear Christians pray, can not fail to have noted that in all these they have confessed enough to have sent them to the state's prison. Christians are always confessing their proneness to sin, "as the sparks are to fly upward." Many of my readers will remember, that, in a former volume,* I turned to the Bible, and exhibited a chapter of the short-comings of its grandest heroes.

The trouble with the Christian system was, and is, *it does not know* how to make good people of its own advocates. Paul has stated the whole matter so clearly and truthfully in Rom. vii. 7–25, that his statement can neither be refuted, nor its "natural force abated." His version of the matter is as follows: —

---

* Question Settled, pp. 37 to 39, published by William White & Co., Boston.

"What shall we say then? Is the law sin? God forbid. Nay, I had not known sin, but by the law: for I had not known lust, except the law had said, Thou shalt not covet. But sin, taking occasion by the commandment, wrought in me all manner of concupiscence. For without the law sin was dead. For I was alive without the law once: but when the commandment came, sin revived, and I died. And the commandment, which was ordained to life, I found to be unto death. For sin, taking occasion by the commandment, deceived me, and by it slew me. Wherefore the law is holy, and the commandment holy, and just, and good. Was then that which is good made death unto me? God forbid. But sin, that it might appear sin, working death in me by that which is good: that sin by the commandment might become exceeding sinful. For we know that the law is spiritual: but I am carnal, sold under sin. For that which I do, I allow not; for what I would, that do I not; but what I hate, that do I. If then I do that which I would not, I consent unto the law that it is good. Now then it is no more I that do it, but sin that dwelleth in me. For I know that in me (that is, in my flesh), dwelleth no good thing: for to will is present with me; but how to perform that which is good I find not. For the good that I would I do not: but the evil which I would not, that I do. Now if I do that I would not, it is no more I that do it, but sin that dwelleth in me. I find then a law, that, when I would do good, evil is present with me. For I delight in the law of God after the inward man: But I see another law in my members, warring against the law of my mind, and bringing me into the captivity to the law of sin which is in my members. O wretched man that I am! who shall deliver me from the body of this death? I thank God through Jesus Christ our Lord. So then with my mind I myself serve the law of God; but with my flesh the law of sin."

I think it impossible for even the most stupid Christian to misapprehend this statement. Paul gives his own experience, his daily conflicts. How hard the struggles of this gospel " Boanerges!" How weak he was when in the power of sin! All his life, this "other law" in his members, bringing him into captivity to the law of sin. Poor "chief of sinners!" All the days of his life going around exclaiming, "Who shall deliver me from the body of this death?" This apostolic sinner never found a power in the gospel or elsewhere strong enough to deliver him. Could anything more clearly demonstrate the utter insignificancy of the Bible and all its plans, so far as saving men from the commission of sin is concerned? The only consolation Paul had above sinners who had not been Christianized he couched in these words: "There is therefore now no condemnation to them which are in Christ Jesus, who walk not after the flesh, but after the Spirit. For the law of the Spirit of life in Christ Jesus hath made me free from the law of sin and death." (Rom. viii. 1, 2.)

Here it is. Paul was in Christ Jesus. Got into him by baptism. (Rom. vi. 3.) There is no condemnation for the sinner who is in Christ. Jesus had paid the penalty for his sins; so, although he was chained to "the body of this death," the spirit of God dwelt in him (Rom. viii. 11), and he was waiting for a peculiar manifestation which he hoped would put him beyond the necessity of sin. (Verses 19-24.) He, however, had in this one consolation; that is, sin, with all its consequences, could not tear him away from the love of God, in Christ Jesus. (Verses 38, 39.)

Our readers will remember the confession of a pious saint, in a previous chapter of this work: "O Lord, I never told a truth in my life, but have continually affirmed for a truth what I knew to be a lie." The confession of modern Christians is, "O Lord, if thou hadst dealt justly by us, we might have been with the rich man in hell calling for water to cool our parched tongues." Thus, in every shape, is the confession made, that so far as making men and women *practically* good in this world is concerned, Bible religion is a failure.

When it is remembered that the Bible everywhere holds up bad examples before its adherents, it could not be expected that even good precepts would greatly advance its adherents in morality. I do not now remember an example in the Bible held up as a specimen of perfection, but the following of it out would convert this world into a worse than Pandemonium. Take, as an illustration, the parables given by Jesus; there is not one of them that does not, in some way, justify the evil and put down the good. In Luke, xv. 11-32, is the parable of the Prodigal Son. I quote it entire:—

"And he said, A certain man had two sons: And the younger of them said to his father, Father, give me the portion of goods that falleth to me. And he divided unto them his living. And not many days after the younger son gathered all together, and took his journey into a far country, and there wasted his substance with riotous living. And when he had spent all, there arose a mighty famine in the land; and he began to be in want. And he went and joined himself to a citizen of that country; and he sent him into the fields to feed swine. And he would fain have filled his belly with the husks that the swine did eat: and no man gave unto him. And when he came to himself, he said, How many hired servants of my father's have bread enough and to spare, and I perish with hunger! I will arise and go to my father, and will say unto him, Father, I have sinned against heaven and before thee, and am no more worthy to be called thy son: make me as one of thy hired servants. And he arose, and came to his father. But when he was yet a great way off, his father saw him, and had compassion, and ran, and fell on his neck, and kissed him. And the son said unto him, Father, I have sinned against heaven, and in thy sight, and am no more worthy to be called thy son. But the father said to his servants, Bring forth the best robe, and put it on him; and put a ring on his hand, and shoes on his feet: And bring hither the fatted calf, and kill it; and let us eat, and be merry: for this my son was dead, and is alive again; he was lost, and is found. And they began to be merry. Now his elder son was in the field: and as he came and drew nigh to the house, he heard music and dancing. And he called one of the servants, and asked what these things meant. And he said unto him, Thy brother is come; and thy father hath killed the fatted calf, because he hath received him safe and sound. And he was angry, and would not go in: therefore came his father out, and entreated him. And he answering said to his father, Lo, these many years do I serve thee, neither transgressed I at any time thy commandment; and yet thou never gavest me a kid, that I might make merry with my friends: but as soon as this thy son was come, which hath devoured thy living with harlots, thou hast killed for him the fatted calf. And he said unto him, Son, thou art ever with me, and all that I have is thine. It was meet that we should make merry, and be glad: for this thy brother was dead, and is alive again; and was lost, and is found."

This parable, whether originally given for that purpose or not, is read and commented on to show God's forgiving disposition, — his willingness to meet the sinner half way, and the particular and especial favor he shows to the greatest sinners. The father is said to represent God, who has been offended by our sins. The human family is divided into two classes, — the outrageously wicked are represented by the prodigal son; the naturally just and virtuous — "just persons that need no repentance" — are represented by the older son. Now, this prodigal son takes half of the old man's estate and squanders it, then returns to get the portion of the estate that justly belongs to his virtuous and otherwise righteous brother. What is the result? The father meets him while he is " yet a great way off," and orders the best robe put on him, his person decked with jewelry, the fatted calf to be killed, a band of music employed, a supper, dancing, and a general good time ensues, and the old man never so much as invites his dutiful son to the party, or even informs him of the return of his wicked brother. When the faithful son would know the meaning of all this, his only chance is to inquire of a field-hand.

He is answered, that his brother has returned, and there is a great feast and dancing-party at his father's house. Was he not justly indignant? His father, notwithstanding all his faithful services, had never so much as given him a kid, or even a dish of kid soup; and now all this ado over a profligate brother was an outrage, and would be justly resented by any worthy young man in the country.

Bible Christians will agree with me, that the old man was unjust to his oldest son. Not one of them would follow his example. The claim is, that God has a right to thus deal with his children. I deny it. Spiritualism denies it, and pronounces it a piece of outrageous injustice. This harmonizes with, and was undoubtedly gotten up to illustrate the idea, that the greater the sinner in this world, the greater the saint in the next, — the more one sins here, the more will he be forgiven, and consequently the happier one will be in the next world. Jesus illustrates this by reference to a case who had been a terrible sinner. He says, "Wherefore I say unto thee, Her sins, which are many, are forgiven; for she loved much: but to whom little is forgiven, the same loveth little. And he said unto her, Thy sins are forgiven." (Luke vii. 47.)

The Parable of the Unjust Steward reads as follows: "And he said also unto his disciples, There was a certain rich man, who had a steward; and the same was accused unto him that he had wasted his goods. And he called him, and said unto him, How is it that I hear this of thee? give an account of thy stewardship; for thou mayest be no longer steward. Then the steward said within himself, What shall I do? for my lord taketh away from me the stewardship: I cannot dig; to beg I am ashamed. I am resolved what to do, that, when I am put out of the stewardship, they may receive me into their houses. So he called every one of his lord's debtors unto him, and said unto the first, How much owest thou unto my lord? And he said, A hundred measures of oil. And he said unto him, Take thy bill, and sit down quickly, and write fifty. Then said he to another, And how much owest thou? And he said, A hundred measures of wheat. And he said unto him, Take thy bill, and write fourscore. And the lord commended the unjust steward because he had done wisely: for the children of this world are in their generation wiser than the children of light. And I say unto you, Make to yourselves friends of the mammon of unrighteousness; that, when ye fail, they may receive you into everlasting habitations."

These plain declarations need but little, if any, comment. The steward was a scoundrel, and finally made hosts of friends by cheating his master in settling with those who owed him. Then follows one of the lessons that Jesus would teach by this parable: "And the lord commended the unjust steward because he had acted wisely," and then condemns the "children of light" for not imitating the example of the knave he introduces as a hero. Now follows his advice to his disciples: "And I say unto you, make to yourselves friends of the mammon of unrighteousness, that when ye fail, they may receive you into everlasting habitations." (Verse 9.) Could there be a more positive command to play the rogue's part than is there expressed? Should such a piece of advice be found in the writings of A. J. Davis or Victoria C. Woodhull, what would be the result? Every Christian paper in the United States would reproduce it, with comments to show the immoral tendency of Spiritualism. How strange! We will admire, and even *reverence* things in the Bible, that we could not be induced to tolerate in a person of this age.

The Parable of the Unjust Judge reads as follows: " And he spake a parable unto them to this end, that men ought always to pray, and not to faint; saying, There was in a city a judge, which feared not God, neither regarded man: and there was a widow in that city; and she came unto him, saying, Avenge me of mine adversary. And he would not for a while: but afterward he said within himself, Though I fear not God, nor regard man; yet because this widow troubleth me, I will avenge her, lest by her continual coming she weary me. And the Lord said, Hear what the unjust judge saith. And shall not God avenge his own elect, which cry day and night unto him, though he bear long with them? I tell you that he will avenge them speedily. Nevertheless, when the Son of man cometh, shall he find faith on the earth? And he spake this parable unto certain which trusted in themselves that they were righteous, and despised others." (Luke xviii. 1-9.)

In the Orthodox interpretation of this parable (which is the only correct one), God is represented as being the unjust judge; those who pray, are represented by the widow who *teased* the judge? The leading idea is, that God, whom we are to follow in all things, will not consult justice in answering prayers, but will answer without any reference to the right, in order to get rid of the worrying troubles caused by the continual praying of his children. If God answers prayer at all, the idea is certainly a true one. No person ever asked God to do anything for him without either implying that God would not do his duty by him without his prayers, and hence that God is an unjust judge, or that he wants something that God could not, in justice, give; and now he will either play the part of a spoiled child, and tease God's life out of him, or compel him, by his teasing, to an act of injustice. Now, I ask in all candor and sincerity, can any interpretation be put on the parable of the unjust judge that will allow that the one who originated it knew anything of the first principles of justice? The fact is, the only idea contained in the parable is, that God will sacrifice justice in answer to the prayers of his children.

Though an instructive lesson might be learned from every one of Jesus' parables, I will only occupy space with one more. "For the kingdom of heaven is like unto a man that is a householder, which went out early in the morning to hire laborers into his vineyard. And when he had agreed with the laborers for a penny a day, he sent them into his vineyard. And he went out about the third hour, and saw others standing idle in the market-place, and said unto them, Go ye also into the vineyard, and whatsoever is right I will give you. And they went their way. Again he went out about the sixth and ninth hour, and did likewise. And about the eleventh hour he went out, and found others standing idle, and saith unto them, Why stand ye here all the day idle? They say unto him, Because no man hath hired us.

He saith unto them, Go ye also into the vineyard; and whatsoever is right, that shall ye receive. So when even was come, the lord of the vineyard saith unto his steward, Call the laborers, and give them their hire, beginning from the last unto the first. And when they came that were hired about the eleventh hour, they received every man a penny. But when the first came, they supposed that they should have received more; and they likewise received every man a penny. And when they had received it, they murmured against the goodman of the house, saying, These last have wrought but one hour, and thou hast made them equal unto us, which have borne the burden and heat of the day. But he answered one of them, and said, Friend, I do thee no wrong: didst not thou agree with me for a penny? Take that thine is, and go thy way: I will give unto this last, even as unto thee. Is it not lawful for me to do what I will with mine own? Is thine eye evil, because I am good? (Matt. xx. 1–15.)

Now I think any jury, bound upon their honor, would decide, if these men who had "borne the burden and heat of the day," had sued this householder, that this was a case of outrageous injustice. It occurs to me that this man took advantage of these poor laborers, who were out of employment, when he hired them for a penny a day. Indeed, he virtually confesses this himself, when he promised others that he would pay them "whatsoever was right" for one hour's work, and then paid them a penny. If it was right to give them a penny for one hour's labor in the cool of the day, it certainly was not right to compel the others to work full twelve hours, and "bear the burden and heat of the day," and then pay them off with a penny. No one claims that this is justice between man and man.

The explanation given of this parable is, that it illustrates God's goodness in saving sinners on a dying bed. God is the householder, the field is the world. Men and women are the laborers. The parable is given to show that God will give the same reward in heaven to the villain who becomes his servant at the last hour of his life, as to the one who spends a lifetime in his service. The explanation does not help the matter; even that is unjust and unfair. God has no right to war against the moral interest of his children here in any such way. The religion which teaches that God would thus deal by his children, not only teaches them to imitate this God in this example, in their dealings with each other, but holds out inducements for them to enjoy, what Paul would call, "the pleasures of sin, for a season;" as they will be just as happy in heaven by serving God but one hour. Spiritualism rejects the leading sentiment of each of these parables, fully believing that they are calculated to lower the standard of morality among the people.

THE BIBLE ABOUNDS IN PRECEPTS, THE CARRYING OUT OF WHICH MUST MORALLY DEGRADE THE PEOPLE.

Beyond all doubt, the Bible has many good maxims, axioms, and precepts. If there were none in it that tended in any other direction, a moderately good life could be lived in harmony with its teachings; but, alas! too many of its precepts, if obeyed, would render the world so much worse than it is, that all would soon demand the abolition of the Bible from respectable society. A historian says, "And the children of Israel did according to the word of Moses; and they borrowed of the Egyptians jewels of silver and jewels of gold, and raiment: and the Lord gave the people favor in the sight of the Egyptians, so that they lent unto them such things as they required: and they spoiled the Egyptians." (Exod. xii. 35, 36.)

This "spoiling of the Egyptians," was done in obedience to a command of God found in Exodus iii. 22, and xi. 2. In answer to the charge that this was a piece of flagrant injustice, the defenders of the Bible usually urge that the children of Israel were slaves, and it was but just that they should have the property they obtained by this "breach of trust," under God's command, as a compensation for their labors.

Much capital has been made out of the slavery of the children of Israel in Egypt, but, like many other arguments of the clergy, it is untrue. In the sense that the children of Israel may have been regarded as foreigners and not citizens they may have been slaves, but beyond that were no more enslaved than are the working classes generally. They were freeholders colonized together, and had their lands, cattle, and sheep in the most fertile parts of Egypt. (Gen. xlvii. 11, 27; Exod. ix. 4–6; x. 23, 26; xii. 23, 27, 32, 38.)

Deut. xiv. 21, contains the following bad precept; "Ye shall not eat of anything that dieth of itself: thou shalt give it unto the stranger that is in thy gates, that he may eat it; or thou mayest sell it unto an alien: for thou art a holy people unto the Lord thy God. Thou shalt not seethe a kid in his mother's milk."

Is this just? If that which died of itself was fit to eat, then the command not to eat it was wrong; if it was not fit to eat, then it was wrong to sell or give it to any one else to eat. The religion of Spiritualism could not recognize the justice of anything of the kind.

Deut. xiii. 6-11, reads as follows: "If thy brother, the son of thy mother, or thy son, or thy daughter, or the wife of thy bosom, or thy friend, which is as thine own soul, entice thee secretly, saying, Let us go and serve other gods which thou hast not known, thou, nor thy fathers; namely, of the gods of the people which are round about you, nigh unto thee, or far off from thee, from the one end of the earth even unto the other end of the earth. Thou shalt not consent unto him nor hearken unto him; neither shall thine eye pity him, neither shalt thou spare, neither shalt thou conceal him. But thou shalt surely kill him: thine hand shall be first upon him to put him to death, and afterwards the hand of all the people. And thou shalt stone him with stones, that he die; because he hath sought to thrust thee away from the Lord thy God, which brought thee out of the land of Egypt, from the house of bondage."

Here husbands are commanded to kill wives; brothers, brothers; fathers and mothers, their sons and daughters, and friends, bosom friends, for a difference in religious opinion. Spiritualists urge the utmost liberality in religious opinion, and Spiritualism forbids any one the right to kill for any purpose whatever, much less for a difference of religious faith. The truth is, the churches themselves have outgrown many things in the Bible.

Deut. xxi. 18-21 says, "If a man have a stubborn and rebellious son, which will not obey the voice of his father, or the voice of his mother, and that, when they have chastened him, will not hearken unto them: then shall his father and his mother lay hold on him, and bring him out unto the elders of his city, and unto the gate of his place; and they shall say unto the elders of his city, This our son is stubborn and rebellious, he will not obey our voice; he is a glutton and a drunkard. And all the men of his city shall stone him with stones, that he die: so shalt thou put evil away from among you; and all Israel shall hear, and fear."

Is this the way to treat a badly organized child, — one that did not organize himself, and was no more to blame for being "stubborn, rebellious, and a drunkard," than the sun is for shining, or rain for falling? If there is any blame anywhere, it is with the parents who gave him his organism, and the society that called out the latent incongruities and failed to develop the normal action of his organism. Let us spare the child, and throw around him more harmonious conditions, we may then enable him, in the next world, to be

"—— blest with a holier birth
Than the passions of man allowed him on earth."

The command to murder such an unfortunately organized child is not good. Spiritualism would *bless*, and not kill this poor, unfortunately organized child.

In Leviticus xxv. 44-46, is a passage of Scripture that has been used with crushing effect by the American slave-monger. It reads as follows: "Both thy bondmen, and thy bondmaids, which thou shalt have, shall be of the heathen that are round about you ; of them shall ye buy bondmen and bondmaids. Moreover, of the children of the strangers that do sojourn among you, of them shall ye buy, and of their families that are with you, which they begat in your land; and they shall be your possession. And ye shall take them as an inheritance for your children after you, to inherit them for a possession; they shall be your bondmen forever: but over your brethren, the children of Israel, ye shall not rule one over another with rigor."

How many hundreds of times, and with what cursed effects, has this precious bit of " God's Holy Word," been used in this country, to tighten the chains of the " divine institution " of slavery upon the millions of innocent victims that were so many years held in bondage. I am personally acquainted with hundreds of people who were led astray by this very text. Thousands of innocent rebels went into the late war fully believing that God would miraculously interfere in behalf of the " divine institution." Some who were conscientiously opposed to slavery, when their ministers in the South showed them how clearly the Bible taught that they were in the right and abolitionists in the wrong, yielded their opposition, and laid down their lives in behalf of " the sum of all villanies."

Not only did " the Book of books," their moral and religious guide, give them the privilege of owning slaves, but to beat them, and under certain circumstances to kill them ; that is to whip them so that they would die within a few days.

Here is the law on that subject. " And if a man

smite his servant, or his maid, with a rod, and he die under his hand, he shall be surely punished. Notwithstanding, if he continue a day or two, he shall not be punished; for he is his money." (Exod. xxi. 20, 21.)

Such texts need no comment, and I offer none. I only say, the book that contains them must be an imperfect guide to holiness.

In Num. xxxi. 17, 18, is a command, which, to say the least, is not very elevating in its moral character. It reads as follows: "Now, therefore, kill every male among the little ones, and kill every woman that hath . . . but all the women children that hath not . . . keep alive for yourselves."

Such language needs no comment. Ministers have used a great deal of lung force, and bundles upon bundles of quills have been used up, to try to convince the world that this command is not bad; but the world is not yet convinced. The command is an outrage on our sense of justice; present inspiration can give better ones.

In Prov. xxxi. 6, 7, Solomon, the wise man, is represented as saying, " Give strong drink unto him that is ready to perish, and wine unto those that be of heavy hearts. Let him drink and forget his poverty, and remember his misery no more."

How much "strong drink" does it take to enable the poor man to forget his poverty? How much will it take to keep him in a condition where he will remember his misery no more? I have seen poor men get rich on twenty-five cents, but to keep so would require the investment of a good many dollars.

The New Testament is a decided improvement on the Old, yet it contains many silly, and some absolutely wicked commands. In Matt. vi. 25-34, is a department of Jesus' great Sermon on the Mount. It reads as follows: "Therefore I say unto you, Take no thought for your life, what ye shall eat, or what ye shall drink; nor yet for your body, what ye shall put on. Is not the life more than meat, and the body than raiment? Behold the fowls of the air: for they sow not, neither do they reap, nor gather into barns; yet your heavenly Father feedeth them. Are ye not much better than they? Which of you by taking thought can add one cubit unto his stature? And why take ye thought for raiment? Consider the lilies of the field, how they grow; they toil not, neither do they spin: and yet I say unto you, that even Solomon in all his glory was not arrayed like one of these. Wherefore, if God so clothe the grass of the field, which to-day is, and to-morrow is cast into the oven, shall he not much more clothe you, O ye of little faith? Therefore take no thought, saying, What shall we eat, or, what shall we drink? or, wherewithal shall we be clothed? (for after all these things do the Gentiles seek): for your heavenly Father knoweth that ye have need of all these things. But seek ye first the kingdom of God, and his righteousness; and all these things shall be added unto you. Take therefore no thought of the morrow; for the morrow shall take thought for the things of itself. Sufficient unto the day is the evil thereof."

What would a minister think of a church that would harbor one serious thought of obeying this text? His first conclusion would be, that he would be compelled to look somewhere else for his salary. Obedience to this text would of course lead to vagrancy, with all its attendant crimes. When men and women, in obedience to this text, live as the birds do, without plowing, sowing, or gathering into barns, the millennium will come in the shape of pandemonium. This command, if not wicked, is foolish.

In Matt. x. 34–38, Jesus says, " Think not that I am come to send peace on earth; I came not to send peace, but a sword. For I am come to set a man at variance against his father, and the daughter against her mother, and the daughter-in-law against her mother-in-law, and a man's foes shall be they of his own household. He that loveth father and mother more than me is not worthy of me; and he that loveth son and daughter more than me is not worthy of me. And he that taketh not his cross and followeth after me is not worthy of me."

In these days of spirit manifestations, we hear a great deal of talk about Spiritualism breaking up families. Professors Mattison, Mahan, *et al.*, thought that nothing good could sow the devastation and desolation that grew in the wake of Spiritualism. Can it be worse than that which Jesus advertised as his work? The chief intention of the hero of Christianity was not to sow peace and harmony in families, but its opposite. As Jehovah was a jealous God, and would not tolerate the interference of other gods (see Exod. xxxiv. 14–16), so Jesus was even jealous of a mother's love for a child, or a husband's love for his wife. If a child loved father or mother more than it did Jesus, it was unworthy of him. In Luke xiv. 26, the language is stronger than that already quoted. There Jesus says, —

" If any man come to me and hate not his father and mother, and wife and children, and brethren and sisters, yea, and his own life also, he cannot be my disciple."

Now I am led to ask, Can a book teaching such sentiments, in the first sense of the word, be moral? Even though we submit to the claim of the clergy, and interpret the word hate, as can not honestly be done, to mean "love less," is it just to ask me to love that wife, who in her youth forsook all for me, and has ever since done her whole duty by me, *less* than I love Jesus; and what of those children which are the result of the union of her soul and mine? Must I love those whose very existence I am responsible for less than I love Jesus, who certainly has no more claims to my love than have the revolutionary heroes who laid down their lives for my liberty? It is unjust to ask me to love Jesus above all others. I can not do it.

One more text is enough to show the imperfections of biblical precepts. John, the beloved disciple of Jesus, says, "If there come any unto you and bring not this doctrine, receive him not into your house, neither bid him God speed." (2 John i. 10.)

Is this a good precept? Suppose that the mercury was at this hour twenty degrees below zero; and suppose, Christian reader, that I, contaminated by Spiritualism as I am, was to drive up to your house in almost a frozen condition, would you receive me into your house? Or would you first question me concerning my religious faith? Is not the precept, which would freeze me to death because of my honest convictions, a bad one? Would not the Bible be a better book if that was not in it? Would *you* not like it better if all the precepts I have just quoted could be expunged? Spiritualism does not believe them, does not tolerate them, even though they are in the Bible. It calls upon its head, a great deal of opposition on account of its repugnancy to these biblical immoralities. Is not Spiritualism, in this respect, morally ahead of the Bible?

MANY OF THE DOCTRINES OF THE BIBLE ARE MORALLY DEGRADING IN THEIR TENDENCY.

I have only space under this heading to mention a few points that do not come up in other departments of this book.

Any doctrine that teaches man that the consequences of his acts are not to be visited on him personally, will teach him to act without reference to personal consequences. What could more effectually do this than the present system of religion called Christianity? The Christian system does not teach that a person can be justified by any merits or acts of his own, but, on the contrary, that good actions or works are not recommendations to the favor of the great I AM; on the contrary, it is the belief of a creed or dogma, rather than nobility of character, that is to commend us to the favor of their God and Christ. Paul says, "Being justified freely by his grace through the redemption that is in Christ Jesus, whom God hath set forth to be a propitiation through faith in his blood, to declare his righteousness for the remission of sins that are past, through the forbearance of God; to declare, I say, at this time his righteousness: that he might be just, and the justifier of him which believeth in Jesus. Therefore we conclude that a man is justified by faith without the deeds of the law." (Rom. iii. 24–28.)

Language could not possibly be plainer than this. The *propitiation*, and not honor, integrity, or virtue, is to do the work. He who believes, *is to be justified by faith without the works of, or obedience to, the law.* Is not this calculated to lead *from*, rather than *to* obedience to moral law? I could not, with the stake before me, decide otherwise.

In Rom. iv. 4-8, Paul argues the question still further. Hear him. "Now to him that worketh is the reward not reckoned of grace, but of debt. But to him that worketh not, but believeth on him that justifieth the ungodly, his faith is counted for righteousness. Even as David also describeth the blessedness of the man, unto whom God imputeth righteousness without works, saying, Blessed are they whose iniquities are forgiven, and whose sins are covered. Blessed is the man to whom the Lord will not impute sin."

If the sentence, "But to him that worketh not, but believeth on him that justifieth the ungodly, his faith is counted for righteousness," is not calculated to put righteousness at a discount and ungodliness above par, then language fails to convey any meaning.

Once more, this same apostle explains the matter as follows: "For by grace are ye saved through faith; and that not of yourselves; it is the gift of God; not of works, lest any man should boast. (Eph. ii. 8, 9.)

Nothing could be plainer. Your future destiny is not shaped by yourself, but is purely a work of grace or favor — a gift bestowed on the believer of certain tenets, entirely irrespective of anything done or left undone.

Even the God of the Bible, who, of course, is held

up as an example to his children in all things, is represented as angry. (Psalms ii. 12; vii. 1.) Passionate. (Exod. xxxii. 10.) Weak. (Exod. xxxi. 17; Judges i. 18.) Vascillating. (Gen. vi. 5, 7; Exod. xxxii. 14; Jonah iii. 10.)

I submit, that in proportion as the Bible inspires respect for the character here represented as God, it will incline people to imitate that character. Persons denying the infallibility of the Bible, and looking to the philosophy developed in modern Spiritualism as an aid to overcome the wickedness of the world, will have a better opportunity to learn and practice lessons of morality. While the time spent in the study and imitation of the character of this God is worse than thrown away, that spent in investigating and practicing the laws of life, as developed in Spiritualism, must, as I shall show, result in the redemption of the race.

THE DIFFERENCE.

Having now shown some of the imperfections of the Bible, and its plan for reforming the world, I propose to exhibit some of the superiorities of Spiritualism in that direction. That the phenomena of Spiritualism in itself is calculated to make men better, cannot be disputed. The spiritual phenomena always appeals to the highest qualities of man's nature, — that is, to his social nature. A mother's influence over a child in earth-life is of course designed for good, and if properly used, must tend toward the moral and intellectual development of the child. Even the watch care of the mother will put the child on its guard; so will a belief that fathers, mothers, brothers, and sisters, on the other side of death's narrow stream, incline men to virtue in this life; yet it is not claimed that this is the chief superiority of Spiritualism over opposing religions. Spiritualism and Spiritualists have learned that the world cannot be reformed by precepts. The trial of that has been quite sufficient. The world needs more to be shown how to put into practice the good that it knows than it does an urging to obey precepts of any kind. It does but little good to inform a drowning man that he can be saved by swimming to the shore. No one on the shore knows better than he that there is salvation for him on the shore. All he wants is instruction and ability to get to the shore.

The gospel, as I have shown, failed to teach its adherents how to perform the right. Paul said, "How to perform that which is good, I find not." The world needs teaching more than commanding. Dissertations on the folly or misery of sin, or on "the beauty of holiness," will never save the world. The drunkard knows the evils of intemperance better than the temperance lecturer can point them out. He knows whisky robs him of his brains and fills him with devils and hells, but like Paul, "when he would do good evil is present with him." The thing needed is a system of philosophy, the carrying out of which will naturally, and apparently without effort, make the world better.

Churches have been preaching of *regeneration* as the panacea for all the wickedness there is in the world. Spiritualists, having tested the matter in those professing to have passed that ordeal, have made the important discovery that no *re*-generation can overcome the faults imparted at the first generation. They have learned that if you would have the man right, you must have the child right; and if you would have the child right, you must have him begotten under the right circumstances, of parents properly mated, and at the right time; and then certain conditions must be thrown around the mother during the period of gestation.

Spiritualists have learned that one kind of food will make one kind of head, heart, and muscle, and another kind of food another; that if you wish to make a hog of your child, but little effort is needed more than to feed him plenty of hog, and let him live as much like a hog as possible. Precepts and example can not make an evenly balanced child of one who lives after the example named above. Feed persons properly at proper times, in such quantities as they need of the food they need; give them the right kind of beds, in large, properly ventilated rooms; give them proper quantities of sleep, at the proper hours, with their bodies properly inclined, and their heads in the right direction, and you will, in two generations, *cure* depravity in man, and the churches of the doctrine of total depravity. Thus you will have overcome the necessity for any other kind of preaching than can be done by the village schoolmaster.

The investigation of the spiritual phenomena and development of its philosophy, has opened the door to the investigation of the varied sciences coming under the names, Magnetism, Mesmerism, Clairvoyance, Electricity, Psychometry, and Psychology. The investigation of these and kindred sciences developed by Spiritualism, has taught us that everything in the universe has polarity, or, in other words, a north and south pole,—a positive and negative force. We have also learned that everything is harmonious, or what is generally called good, in proportion as it harmonizes with nature. At night, when darkness reigns, nature sleeps: that is the proper time for persons who would be harmonious to sleep. If you will sleep when nature sleeps, with your north side or end to nature's north, permitting your south to correspond with nature's south, you will be more harmonious with nature, and thus will be enabled to blend with her more perfectly and receive her instructions to a better advantage than you possibly can by any other means. When you perfectly blend with nature you will be in harmony with yourself; then you are what the world calls evenly balanced. In that condition you could not kill, rob, steal, get mad, or in any way wrong any one. The person who is properly brought into the world and lives thus, naturally reads and interprets correctly nature's great infallible volume, he can not go astray. Nothing is more needed in our colleges now than professors who shall thoroughly understand and teach the science of reform — of living truly. These things can not be brought about in a single day. "The mills of the gods grind slowly, but grind exceeding small." Let Spiritualism work after the plan it is now so successfully inaugurating, and in a few thousand years the long looked-for "good time coming" will be here.

I can not better close this chapter than by presenting a summary of the issue between Christians and Spiritualists in the form of a few

SYLLOGISTIC ARGUMENTS.

PROPOSITION. *Resolved*, That the religion of modern Spiritualism is better calculated to morally, mentally, and spiritually elevate humanity, than that of the Bible.

SYLLOGISM NO. 1.

1. That which places good works second to anything else can not, in the first sense of the word, be morally elevating.
2. But the Bible gives moral obligations, or good works, only a secondary position.
3. Therefore the Bible is not, in the first sense of the word, calculated to morally elevate mankind. Proof — Eph. ii. 8, 9; Rom, iii. 20–28.

SYLLOGISM NO. 2.

1. That which loves sin can not be morally elevating.
2. But the gospel does love sin.
3. Therefore the gospel is not morally elevating. Proof — Rom. vi. 17.

SYLLOGISM NO. 3.

1. That which can not teach a person how to do right, can not morally elevate him.
2. But the Bible can not teach a person how to perform that which is right.
3. Therefore the Bible can not morally elevate its adherents. Proof — Rom. vii. 14–25.

SYLLOGISM NO. 4.

1. That which teaches that persons may escape the

consequences of their own acts will teach them to act without reference to consequences.

2. But the Bible does teach that persons may escape the consequences of their acts.

3. Therefore the Bible teaches its adherents to act without reference to consequences. Proof — 1 John i. 7; ii. 1, 2.

SYLLOGISM NO. 5.

1. That which leads to war, rapine, and the shedding of blood, is immoral in its tendency.

2. But the Bible has ever led its followers to war and bloodshed.

3. Therefore the Bible is immoral in its tendency. Proof — The whole history of the church. Numb. xxxi. 1, 7–17; Jer. xlviii. 10; Joel iii. 10–14; Luke xxii. 36.

SYLLOGISM NO. 6.

1. That which warns against education and philosophy is mentally depressing.

2. But the Bible does warn against education and philosophy.

3. Therefore the Bible is calculated to mentally depress its adherents. Proof — 1 Cor. xi. 1–4; Col. ii. 8; 1 Cor. xiv. 38.

SYLLOGISM NO. 7.

1. That which urges an individual to hate and forsake his own family is immoral.

2. But the Bible urges men to forsake and hate their families.

3. Therefore the Bible is immoral. Proof — Matt x. 34–38; Luke xiv. 26.

SYLLOGISM NO. 8.

1. That which leads to intemperance is immoral.
2. The Bible leads to intemperance.
3. Therefore the Bible is immoral. Proof— Deut. xiv. 26; Prov. xxxi. 6; 1 Tim. v. 23.

SYLLOGISM NO. 9.

1. That which teaches that our most secret actions and thoughts are liable at any time to be read to the multitude, will teach its adherents to so act and think that they may be willing that their thoughts and acts may be thus read.
2. But Spiritualism teaches that media can and often do read our acts and thoughts.
3. Therefore it teaches its adherents to see that even its secret acts and thoughts are pure. Proof— The whole spiritual phenomena.

SYLLOGISM NO. 10.

1. That which teaches that each individual must abide the consequences of his or her own acts, will teach its adherents to act with reference to consequences.
2. But Spiritualism does teach that each individual must abide the consequences of his or her own acts.
3. Therefore Spiritualism teaches its adherents to so act that they may be willing to take, in their own persons, the consequences of every act. Proof— All the spiritual literature of the nineteenth century.

In conclusion of this chapter permit me to say, that

if Spiritualism boasts of one thing more than another, it is its eclecticism, its optimism. It takes

"—— truth wherever found,
Whether on Christian or on heathen ground."

The Quaker poet, in his contrast of the Old and New, thus apostrophizes the New:—

"For still the new transcends the old,
In signs and tokens many fold:
Slaves rise up men; the olive waves,
With roots deep set in battle graves.

"Through the harsh noises of the day
A low, sweet prelude finds its way;
Through clouds of doubt and creeds of fear,
A light is breaking calm and clear.

"Henceforth my heart shall sigh no more
For olden time and holier shore;
God's love and blessing, then and there,
Are now, and here, and everywhere!"

That writer and readers may be enabled to bring into every-day practice the best good of all religions, is my most sincere desire.

CHAPTER IV.

THE MISSION OF SPIRITUALISM.

Spiritualism necessarily iconoclastic. — A superior Light. — Jesus *vs.* Moses. — The world's Light and Saviours. — Relation of Spiritualism to Christianity. — The decay of Institutions. — Babylon, Greece, Rome. — Republicanism as it was and is. — All stationary Institutions doomed. — The Good of all preserved. — A moving World. — A glance at the Christian World. — "What went ye out for to see." — A lethargic State. — The Infidel World. — A Feast of Negatives. — Dominion of Orthodoxy. — Programme changed. — Ministers on their good Behavior. — A Thought awakener. — The Hydesville Manifestations. — The *Vox Populi.* — Table Tippings. — New Theories of explanation. — Writing Mediumship. — A new set of Thoughts awakened. — — Entrancement. — Sublimity of the Subject. — Efforts to confound the Media. — Opposers confounded. — A change of Base. — A new element of success. — A Hearing obtained. — Number of its Adherents. — Elements of Success. — Not a Matter of Faith. — Quality of Spiritualists. — Their Happiness. — Questions for Skeptics. — Death and the Grave destroyed. — An outside Work. — A few Words with Spiritualists. — A Bid for your Spiritualism. — Our Duty.

ALTHOUGH there never was, nor ever can be, a word written in defence of Spiritualism, but that must to some extent point out its mission, a chapter devoted especially to an elucidation of that subject may not be amiss. Though Spiritualism may have hitherto appeared almost exclusively *iconoclastic*, it is not so; its chief object is not to tear down, but to build. In clearing the foundations of a new superstructure it is sometimes necessary to remove the ruins and rubbish of old dilapidated ones. The sun does not shine on purpose to put the moon and stars to shame; yet the more effulgent light of the sun has always so dimmed the lesser lights that they might have become jealous, and urged that the naughty sun only shines to obscure them. They could have said its work is purely that of an incendiary; see, it has totally obscured our light! How dreadful! The millions who walked by our light last night must now be deprived of that blessed privilege!

Jesus did not come into the world to fight Judaism, — to overthrow it by positive combat, — but to *outshine* it; this Christians think he did. He showed his own superiority, and that of all who were guided by the light that shone from and through his inspirations, and a similar one coming to themselves, to any books that were ever written. Indeed, so far as books printed with ink on paper were concerned, Jesus was never backward in expressing his infidelity. Did he quote Moses, he more frequently quoted him to dispute his words than otherwise. Moses had said, "An eye for an eye and a tooth for a tooth;" but Jesus could not indorse the sayings of the inspired Moses. He followed this quotation with a disjunctive, "*But I say unto you, resist not evil.*" Did he quote the command, "Thou shalt not kill," he read it only to show its imperfection, — that if man could be kept from being angry with his brother without cause, he would not need any such command. He warned the people, that except their righteousness should exceed the righteousness of the Scribes and Pharisees, whose righteousness consisted in strict obedience to the letter of the Old Testament, they could not enter into the kingdom of heaven. The command, "Thou shalt not commit adultery," he thought could be rendered useless by man becoming so spiritual as to have all lust taken out of his heart. Moses had given certain laws concerning divorce; Jesus did not indorse them. Thus this great teacher takes up one command after another of the Old Testament, and either suggests an improvement, or comes out squarely in opposition to them.

All this might lead some one to ask, "But if you overthrow the authority of the Scriptures in this way, how will we know what to take for a guide?" All this Jesus answers: "You are the light of the world; a city set upon a hill can not be hid; men do not light a candle and put it under a bushel, but on a candlestick, and it giveth light unto all them that are in the house." Thus he teaches that the world is to get its light from those who have this inspiration, not from books. The world had long been looking for saviors, but Jesus answers that: "Ye are the salt of the earth." Then he portrays the consequence of the salt having lost its savor.

Now, I declare that Spiritualism occupies the same relation to Christianity, that Christianity did to Judaism, and is destined to eclipse Christianity, and inaugurate a new dispensation in the same way.

All institutions in point of time are local, and as every institution of the past has given way to something grander in the future, so all present institutions, even those regarded as the most sacred, must give place to those more perfect, better adapted to the wants of man, that yet lie in the womb of the infinite future. The Babylonian government was better than the one which preceded it; so that of the Medes and Persians was better than that of the Babylonians; but "Mene, Mene, Tekel," was written on that, and it gave way to the still more humane government of Greece. Greece could not always stand. The indomitable Romans swept that government into oblivion, retaining all there was good of it. Thus I might trace the history of nations, and find that the universal law is, the good must be superseded by the better. When the people get ripe for republicanism, a republican government is founded, and tyranny trembles before it. Republicanism as it was, was thought good enough, but it could not long satisfy the ever-progressive march of humanity toward intellectual and spiritual freedom. It had to be remodeled. The Constitution of the United States has already had fifteen amendments, and now there are many who think it sadly needs fifteen more. Thus institutions are passing, and newer, better, and higher ones taking their places. It can not be possible that what is called Christianity can escape this general wreck of institutions. As all that was good of Judaism was brought over and incorporated into the Christian system, so all that is worth preserving in Christianity will be incorporated into all future systems. For several hundred years Christianity, under an outside pressure, has steadily lopped off one after another of its excrescences, until now it could hardly be recognized by an ancient Christian. Yet this work is not finished. There are prunings and graftings for it in the immediate future, which will cause it to lose its identity. While institutions are stationary, a common and true saying is,

THE WORLD MOVES.

The world ever has moved; sometimes it has moved so slowly that we have almost been compelled to look through an entire century to see that it moved at all. For some cause it has moved more in the last twenty-five years than in three centuries prior to that. What is the cause of this? Simultaneously with the introduction of modern Spiritualism into the world, came a general awakening on almost every imaginable subject. A general agitation of thought seems, somehow or other, to connect itself with Spiritualism. In order to see this more perfectly, it may be well for us to take a view of the theological world, or that portion of it called Christian, at the time Spiritualism was introduced. First, let us take

A GLANCE AT THE ORTHODOX WORLD.

No observer can fail to have noted the great change that has overtaken so-called Evangelicalism since 1848. At that time, the staples of orthodoxy were, the doctrine of Original Sin, Total Depravity, an Angry God, Eternal Hell, and salvation from the wrath of this God, the pains of a fiery hell, and the clutches of an almighty personal devil, by virtue of a vicarious atonement. If my readers went to church at all in those days, they went to see a minister dressed in a peculiar style, stuck up in a close-communion pulpit, half way between the floor and the ceiling, one who claimed to be a mouthpiece for Almighty God, divinely called, and sent to denounce the wrath of an offended God upon their unprotected heads. They could, as they sat under his eloquence and logic, see themselves as poor defenseless worms, and God, as a great stogy-boot, raised over them to crush their life out. They went to hear of a "heart deceitful above all things, and desperately wicked;" men and women were compared to "cages filled with unclean and hateful birds;" to "the sea casting up mire and dirt." Thus, from Sunday to Sunday, the people went to hear themselves denounced and abused. For some cause or other, a great change has come "over the spirit of the dreams" of the clergymen. We hear but little now of this solemn folly. Why is it? I answer: the people have grown away from it. Ministers would preach to empty pews if they now preached such nonsense.

The truth is, the world has thoroughly awaked from the lethargy that characterized it forty years ago. Then you went to meeting from Sunday to Sunday to hear the same old sing-song story told in the same old way. It was but little matter to you what the minister preached. You went to church, not for an intellectual or spiritual feast, but because it was your duty. You had to go to church or to hell, and you thought of the two you preferred the former. No minister in those days dared meet the consequences of venturing too far from the "ancient landmarks." Thus they repeated themselves and each other. When the barrel of sermons had been preached out, they could turn it over, knock the other head in, and commence again. One set of sermons would do for father, son, and grandson; and so on, almost *ad infinitum*. The world, with few exceptions, was in a lethargic state, — priests and people alike asleep, — hardly one sufficiently awake to hail the dawn of a new thought.

THE INFIDEL WORLD.

If we turn from the orthodox to the infidel world, we find that, in some respects, in the same condition.

Infidels in those days were not thinking as they are now; the most, if not all of them, seemed perfectly contented with negating the affirmations of orthodoxy. They were building no churches, schools, or colleges; in fact, were doing nothing for the world more than denying almost anything a minister would affirm. Thus one portion of the world was stagnant, and the other on a tread-wheel.

Orthodoxy all this time held a dominion over the mind, scarcely excelled by the Catholic church in its palmiest days. The minister was God Almighty's mouthpiece, his great vicegerent. He dressed, looked, talked, and acted a kind of "stand-aside-for-I-am-holier-than-thou" doctrine, and you granted it. He was a "*Learned Divine*," made of better material than common mortals, had more influence with heaven, was better acquainted with the gods and devils than were the common herds of the human family. When you met him, you took off your hat and made your lowest bow. When he expressed an opinion, it settled the question, especially if it was a theological opinion. If you differed with him, you were inclined to keep that difference to yourself. Few dared brave the world so far as to express a difference of opinion with the theologian who had arisen to any notoriety in the world.

A CHANGE.

Now we see a great change. Men have come to regard the minister as being about as good as an ordinary mortal, provided he behaves as well. If he steps aside from the path of right, his actions are criticised the same as that of any other sinner. Formerly it was not strange to see one minister settled over one congregation for twenty, or even fifty years. Now hearers criticise the dress, manner of address, doctrine, and logic of the discourse so astutely, that few ministers can stand the ordeal. The result is, a change of ministers is required more frequently than before. The church is progressing. Some of its members progress rapidly, some slowly. The minister is too liberal for one portion of the church, not liberal enough for another; and the result of all this is, a general upheaving, a tearing up of the old foundations. But enough of this now. A few more thoughts are in reserve on the subject.

THOUGHT AWAKENED.

A writer once said, "When God lets a thinker loose on the world, let it beware." He might have said, When God lets a *thought* out, let the world take warning. Who can tell what new worlds one seed-thought may bring to light? Let Sir Isaac Newton, Harvey, Kepler, Galileo, Luther, or Jenner get an idea, and they will revolutionize the whole world of thought. Well, the theological world was wrapped in deep slumber, never even dreaming that the work of its renovation was so nigh at hand. When the spirit-raps came in the family of one John D. Fox, at Hydesville, N. Y., they came as an awakener. Be patient, dear reader, and you shall see the result. When the sounds were first heard in the winter of 1848, no one suspected the cause. The thumping on the little pine table, however, awakened the world sufficiently to have it inquire after the cause. All is well. A person who is soundly asleep can not even have his attention attracted by the raps, or inquire after their cause.

The truth is, these raps have startled theologians and scientists from their slumbers enough so they can inquire, What is this? The inquiry itself is the agitation of thought; but who can answer? This is the first time the world has had an opportunity to ask a question, and no one is sufficiently awake to answer. One suggests that it is the devil; another, that it is machinery; and another has his peculiar answer. Men, women, and children rush out to hear the tiny sounds, and to see if they can decipher the cause. The wise and the unwise are alike confounded by it. The theologian begins to search his Bible; the chemist goes into his laboratory; all take their "divining-rods" to see if they can divine the cause of the mysterious sounds. The stories of the raps are published in all the daily and weekly newspapers; those who are curious, and have the means, journey to the Mecca of Spiritualism, to learn what they can of this new phenomenon. Thus the world is aroused. One arrives at one conclusion, and another at another. These contradictory hypotheses rub against each other. A general fight ensues among the contradictory positions of an awakened world. Toe-joints, knee-joints, machinery, electricity, trickery, and *od force* so effectually play the game of Kilkenny cats with each other, that not one of them is left to tell the tale of the destruction of the others. Thus the warfare goes on.

Hundreds that fell in the battle against the new phenomena, soon found themselves resurrected on the other side, and with strength enough to do effective battle against either or all of the contradictory theories brought to bear against it. A circumstance as purely accidental as that of the acorn falling on Sir Isaac

Newton's head, had revealed an intelligence connected with the raps which was first proclaimed by a little girl, who said, "Why, mother, it can hear!" and second, by the same child, "*Only look, mother; it can see as well as hear!*"

For a time the angels seemed content with this single form of manifestation; they did not seem to wish to show us at once all they had in store for their brothers and sisters yet in the flesh; so it was rap, rap, rap, here, there, and everywhere. After the world had investigated the raps sufficiently, as the exclusive form of manifestation, and some had decided in favor and others against them, our spirit friends vouchsafed another form of manifestation. Tables began to manifest a strange disposition to get up from the floor, turn over, and move about the room; and, strange to say, there was an intelligence connected with these forms of manifestation! Tables, chairs, and stools would answer questions that were entirely beyond the ken of any in the room.

Now, the world that supposed it had thoroughly exploded the raps, was called upon for an explanation of this. Alas for the ministry and scientists! A new system of explanation was required, as much so as though it had been an entire, independent science that was to run the gantlet of their investigation. The result was, a new research and a readjustment of their theories to suit the circumstances. Thus, still more thought was awakened. This was enough. The agitation of thought was, in this case, as in others, the beginning of wisdom. The new theories of opposition brought to bear against Spiritualism were as unsuccessful as the old. Spiritualism was a "Banquo's Ghost," that refused to "down," even at the bidding of the ministry.

By this time, the angel world had fully prepared, and were ready to exhibit to the world, a form of manifestation. Mediumistic individuals began to observe hitherto unknown sensations in the muscles of the arm. Soon the arm, in many instances, lost its sense of feeling, and became uncontrolable. In this condition, without the brain or soul of the subject knowing what was to be done, the hand would grasp a pencil and write out a communication, in many instances filled with undoubted tests that the writing came from a dead friend, whose signature was attached to the communication. At other times, though the medium may have been inferior in organism and development, a communication would be written, which, for elegancy of diction, or argumentative power, could not have been equalled by any person present. This caused the world to put its thinking-cap on once more, and many who felt themselves fully competent to explain the raps, or tips, without admitting Spiritual agency, after the earnest inquiry, "What does this mean?" found themselves converts to the spiritual philosophy.

The combination of the rapping, tipping, and writing manifestations were destined to ripen the world for something more sublime, which the angel world had in store. Now comes the deep, unconscious, entrancement. Little boys and girls, some of them hardly in their teens, found themselves suddenly thrown into an unconscious state by the new power, and in this condition would arise and give utterance to truths the most grand that ever fell from mortal lips. The sublimity, eloquence, and logic of the discourses had never been surpassed, seldom equaled. Those who had only been attracted to Spiritualism before as a series of phenomena, were now attracted on account of the profound interest they felt in the facts and philosophy that were being uttered by those whom every one knew were entirely ignorant of either. As the most sublime strains of praise issued from the mouths of these "babes," tears chased each other down the cheeks of those unused to weeping; and men and women began to exclaim, as in days of yore, "Truly, they speak as never man spake." Learned doctors, lawyers, ministers, and professors in institutions of learning, circumnavigated the range of their lore to find subjects upon which girls, not fourteen years old, could not, under this power, deliver a learned and eloquent speech. This all proved unavailing, so far as confounding the power was concerned; for it showed a like familiarity with all subjects. Their efforts to "confound these mediums in their speech," were as futile as those of their ancient allies to confound the medium who overthrew Judaism. Departed poets returned, and, in strains the most rhythmical and sublime, not only answered every question asked, and solved every mystery presented, but told of their departure from earth, and their birth into a better country.

A CHANGE OF BASE.

Now Spiritualism, which had up to this point stood exclusively on the defensive, assumed the aggressive, and hoary-headed error fell before it like grass before the scythe. It now made a direct attack on systems which had long enough stayed the progress of the world. It bearded the lion in his den, and old errors, which had denied even the right of existence to Spiritualism, had to fight for their lives. From this time forward but few found time to attack Spiritualism; all had more than they could do to defend their own fortifications. Of course Spiritualism now began to spread more rapidly than ever before, for it had not only all the phenomena that had characterized it up to this point of time, but a philosophy to commend it to the judgment of those who think. Its advocates were not compelled to go through a course of from seven to twenty years of study to be ready to enter upon its ministry. It frequently occurred that a fifteen minutes' schooling in a spirit circle was sufficient to prepare its preacher to more than meet any foe.

IT HAS OBTAINED A HEARING.

Spiritualism has not only as a distinctive form of religion gained the attention of the world, and proved its "right to life, liberty, and the pursuit of happiness," but has, somehow or other, succeeded in ingratiating itself into the general favor of the world, until there is little of the world that does not, somehow or other, mix with and recognize it. It is rapidly finding its way into the stories, poems, songs, and all other literature of the age. It is in one way or another being dramatized, and put on the boards in the theatres, and spreading even in the church in every conceivable way. Such books as Gates Ajar, unwittingly indorsing the phenomena and philosophy of Spiritualism, find their way into almost every family, while books written in opposition to Spiritualism seldom pay their publishers.

With regard to the number of converts that Spiritualism has made, I have but little to say. Having personally made no figures on the matter, I am not prepared to speak with definiteness. Calculations have been made varying all the way from nine to fifteen millions. If it was only two millions, or even one million, the work would be wonderful beyond all precedent. Starting out not a quarter of a century since, with no John the Baptist to herald it, no press or preachers to stand up in its defence, not only without a worker in its behalf, but without a believer in the world, and wading through the most dire opposition that any theory ever met; all the prejudices of the world being brought to bear against it; the pulpit and press volunteering their services in the opposition; all manner of honorable and dishonorable means used in the warfare against it,— the existence of a very few Spiritualists is proof of the power of Spiritualism to resist opposition, and, like an old sword, come out of every fight brighter than it went in. Personally I have traveled through thirty-four States and the Canadas, and, with the exception of New Orleans and San Francisco, have preached Spiritualism in every important city in the Union. In nearly every city my audiences have been much larger than those attending any church. Not only do Spiritualists exist, but there are spiritual societies scattered through all our cities, villages, and hamlets; and the "Macedonian" cry still comes in from every quarter of the globe. The demand for first-class lecturers is to-day ten times as great as the supply. This is a proof that the harvest is ripening. The gathering of souls to the great spiritual harvest is to be greatly increased in the future.

THE MISSION OF SPIRITUALISM.

Now Spiritualism is thoroughly advertised; the prejudices have been met and overcome; our presses and ministers are at work; new media, and new forms of mediumship, are being brought into the field; almost every daily paper contains the history of something new connected with Spiritualism. Thus have we greater reason to be encouraged than ever before. Spiritualism has set out to conquer the world, and will not rest until it has accomplished this part of its mission.

Although Spiritualism has done the work I have just designated, I do not think there is one Spiritualist on earth stronger in his faith for the advancement Spritualism has made in the world. The millions of Spiritualists are every one of them converts, either from personal tests to themselves, which would be just as good if no other person had ever received tests, or because they see the harmony of its phenomena and philosophy with all nature. Be it understood, the difference between Spiritualism and all other religions is, other religions are all matters of faith. Spiritualism is not a faith at all; its advocates tell what they *know*, not what they believe. They testify to what they have seen, not to what they have heard that others have seen.

THE QUALITY OF ITS CONVERTS.

Spiritualism, like a reform advocated by an ancient medium, finds more believers among the "common people" than among those who have more of the honor and wealth of this world on which to rely. Yet, while those of "low estate" gladly rally to its standard, there are not a few of those, whose names would be an honor to any cause, in our ranks. Spiritualists are not all fools or fanatics. Among the leading people of the world who have avowed Spiritualism, either in its name or doctrines, or both, may be classed such names as Queen Victoria, Alexander, the Czar of Russia, Napoleon, ex-Emperor of France, the late Lord Brougham, Hon. J. R. Giddings, Senator Sprague, William Lloyd Garrison, the late Governor Talmadge, Hon. R. D. Owen, Judge J. W. Edmonds, Hon. B. F. Wade, the late President Lincoln, and besides more than as many other statesmen, who stand quite as high as those above named, some of the best scientists and philosophers in the world. Thus has Spritualism proven itself adapted to all states and conditions of people. But this is not all. Spiritualism has not come simply to make a few millions of converts, and among them not a few of the greatest men and women on earth, but it is doing a yet nobler and grander work. I am now ready to consider

THE HAPPINESS OF ITS CONVERTS.

On this department of my subject, I only need to appeal to my Spiritualistic readers. They are certainly competent witnesses. They most of them have enjoyed or *endured* all the consolation that could possibly flow from the religions by which they are surrounded. A vast majority of the Spiritualists have come from the churches; many of them have been acceptable preachers in the various sects throughout Christendom. They know just what the various phases of evangelicalism can do for its adherents, having experienced all its consolations. They also know what Spiritualism can do. By a blessed experience, they have learned the difference between faith and knowledge. Then, I ask, are they not competent to testify in this case? Does the skeptical reader object? Very well; then we will put him on the stand. "Out of thine own mouth will I judge thee."

Friend Skeptic, I ask you to answer me a few plain questions.

1. Which would render you the more happy, — to believe that about six thousand years ago, a short-sighted God had made man a pure, good, and just man and woman, but had, at the same time, or before, made a tempter, who had tempted and enticed this sinless couple, so that they had fallen, insomuch that the men we see now are only the ruins, the *wreck*, of a former race; or to believe that man commenced low down in the scale of being, and had arisen to the noble specimens you see in the world to-day, with every prospect for better men in the future?

2. Which do you prefer to believe, — "original sin," "total depravity;" or that man, like the peach, commenced low down in the scale of being, and developed the baser, the so-called evil faculties first, but is progressing, growing better every year, developing, rounding out, so that some day he will stand comparatively perfect?

3. Which would make you the more happy, — to believe in endless hell, or endless progress? Which would you prefer, — to think of your unconverted child, in the other world, as scorching in endless flames, or endlessly progressing toward all that is pure and good?

4. Which would you prefer, — to daily talk with a sainted companion, or beatified parent or child, or know that they were locked up in an orthodox

heaven or hell, with not the least interest in you or yours?

5. Which would you prefer, — to go to an orthodox heaven, knowing that some of your friends were on the road to endless perdition, and the remainder of them suffering all of life's vicissitudes, and you not have the privilege of coming to them, or to take your position in a Spiritualists' "Summer Land," with the privilege of working for, and bringing earth-friends to a purer and better life?

Dear reader, I know we are not to make Spiritualism true or false by popular vote; a theory is not made false or true at our option; yet the answer to these questions will certainly suggest the comparative happiness of those who believe, and those who reject Spiritualism.

Spiritualism has shown us the "Gates Ajar." Our dead are brought back to us. We see them; we talk with them; we enjoy their society. Death has been robbed! His sting is gone! The grave has been despoiled of its victory! Those whom, in times past, we have regarded as locked in the gloomy vault, are not dead. We see them, hear them, and know they are not dead. They are with us, — more than ever ours. Spiritualism has come with all this good news. O glorious religion! May thy banners be unfurled, and thy peaceful influences spread, until all the world shall know thy beauty, and worship at thy feet!

Even this is not the whole of the mission of Spiritualism.

ITS OUTSIDE WORK

is greater, if possible, than anything yet mentioned. Spiritualism has already re-made the religions of the country. Where is the minister who has not re-made his discourses in obedience to its behests? Where is the minister who now preaches a hell of fire and brimstone? What has become of the doctrine of total depravity, with its etceteras? What has become of the anger that rankled so in the bosom of an orthodox God forty years ago? Ah, these things are all gone! What killed them? I answer — *Spiritualism!* The people have had a taste of Spiritualism, and will not turn from it to the husks they have been wont to get from the pulpits. The result is, the ministers have been compelled to re-make their discourses, or preach to empty pews. This will go on until Spiritualism proper will be preached in every pulpit in the land. O glorious day! Speed it, Heaven!

A WORD TO SPIRITUALISTS.

Spiritualists, the work I have spoken of in this chapter, already accomplished, is grand. Our religion has already saved thousands from many miseries in this life, and the tormenting fear of untold agony in the next. Many honest, useful, rational citizens to-day owe their happiness, if not their sanity, to the kindly and timely interference of Spiritualism. Now permit me to ask you, what would you take for your Spiritualism? Suppose I had the money to pay into your hands now, how much would it take to buy you out? Remember, I am to buy your part of Spiritualism, and the work it has done, out of the world! You are not to know that it exists. I am also to buy its indirect influences through the churches and through society over you, so you shall be morally and mentally where you would have been had Spiritualism never been heard of. In its stead a yawning, fiery hell; in short, old theology, with all its devils and goblins grim, shall stare you in the face.

Now you are ready to talk to me. How much will you take for your Spiritualism? Ah, if all the world were in one scale, and Spiritualism and its consequences in the other, I think I see you getting into the scale with Spiritualism. Now, let me tell you, there are thousands in this world to-day, almost, if not quite, where you were before Spiritualism put its tender hands so lovingly under you. Do you realize that every new truth brings new duties? This great spiritual boon came to many of you not only without money and without price, but absolutely unsought, unwanted, and, in not a few instances, unwelcomed. Now it is your privilege to co-operate with the angels, and carry this work forward.

If Spiritualism has made you happy, it is reasonable that it would do the same for your neighbor. Could you not make a little effort to lay it before him? Millions are being squandered every year to send the gospel to the heathen, and millions more are exhausted in preaching a worse than heathenish gospel to your neighbors. You have the power to at least partly counteract that work. Will you do it? If you are alone in this blessed knowledge, will you at least make one thorough effort to get our lectures and literature before your neighbors? If you are not alone, will you co-operate with your brethren in trying to speed this cause in your own immediate vicinity? You may thus be a means of blessing, and being a "savor of life unto life" to others, as you have been blessed, and thus bring a double blessing to your own soul.

THE MISSION OF SPIRITUALISM. 121

The privilege of assisting in this work now, while you are needed, is extended to you. Do, I beseech you, step into this gap. There is not a drone in all the hives of our adversaries. Let us emulate their example.

> "If you can not in the conflict
>   Prove yourself a soldier true —
> If, when fire and smoke are thickest,
>   There's no work for you to do:
> When the battle field is silent,
>   You can go with careful tread, —
> You can bear away the wounded,
>   You can cover up the dead.
>
> "Do not, then, stand idly waiting
>   For some greater work to do;
> Fortune is a lazy goddess —
>   She will never come to you.
> Go and toil in any vineyard;
>   Do not fear to do or dare;
> If you want a field of labor,
>   You can find it anywhere."

That Spiritualists may realize what the angels have done for them, and show their appreciation of this work by a consecration of their all, and concentrated and concerted action in behalf of the truths they love, and that their works may be crowned with more abundant success in the future than in the past, is the most earnest desire of the writer of this volume.

CHAPTER V.

THE CUI BONO OF SPIRITUALISM.

A proper Inquiry.— Its Work slow.— Jesus' Argument.—" By their Fruits shall ye know them."— Author's Experience.— A Struggle with Poverty.— Letter from Dr. Newton.— Reflections on the same.— Author takes Courage. — Dr. Newton's three Months' Work.— Suicide of a Girl.— Her dead Mother kept her from Sin.— Worldly good of Spiritualism.— Serfs liberated.— Lizzie Keizer and the Apple Pedler.— Experience as a Healer.— Cure of a withered Hand.— A Lady saved.— That Bread Fund.— A Medium saved from a Railroad Accident.— A Train of Cars saved by Spirit Interposition.— Peter West saves a Train of Cars.— A Collision avoided.— A Conflagration saved by Spirits.— Pair of Shoes sent to a Beggar.— Inventions by Spirits.— Moral good of Spiritualism.— A Methodist Lady in Trouble.— A Dialogue.— Petty Tyranny.— A Drunkard saved.— A Case in Wisconsin.— Case in Chicago.— Spirits curing Appetite for Tobacco.— A Medium compelled to restore his illgotten Money.— Other Stimulants to Purity.— " Be sure your Sins will find you out."— Mental good of Spiritualism.— Lady saved from Insanity by her Spirit Son.— Asylums cheated out of Subjects.— Case in Iowa.— Only a few Grains.— Spiritualism in a dying Hour.

THOUGH we may not be able at first sight to see all of the good of things newly discovered and developed, and sometimes not any of it, yet it is always proper to inquire after the good of any thing that comes to the world, more especially those that man seems to have some hand in bringing about. It is true that even the advocates of new systems can not always tell the good that is to grow out of them. When Benjamin Franklin was questioned as to the good of his electrical experiments, he confessed that he could not see just what good would come from them. Ask our telegraphic operators, or any one who knows anything of the workings of the Atlantic cable, and they will tell you the good of past experiments with the electric forces.

It is conceded that a new theory, calculated to supplant old institutions and not put something better in their place, can not work for the benefit of humanity. He is a villian who would tear down your house, and leave you without shelter in the street. He who would persuade you to leave your house for a better one, you would class among your best friends. So, if Spiritualism has come simply to tear down old institutions, and raze the foundations on which society is built, and not put something better in their place, its work is purely that of an incendiary; the quicker it meets its doom the better for the world. Yet it must be remembered that large bodies move slowly. " The Pyramids were not built in a day," nor do revolutions always spring into life and accomplish their work in a few weeks.

It may be that the inquiry the world is now making after the good already accomplished by Spiritualism, is just a little premature. Though Spiritualism has always been in the world, it is not yet a quarter of a century since it commenced the work of forcing itself upon the public mind as a distinctive religion. It has had no standing armies, no political parties to enforce its tenets upon the people. It may not, in twenty-four years, have accomplished so much good as Christianity has in the centuries of its dominion, yet that is offset by the fact that it has not done so much evil. It has not founded many institutions of learning, neither has it produced a Saint Bartholomew's Day, where *one hundred thousand* lives were sacrificed to its chief Mogul in a single day. Thus it may not have done as much work as older religions. It takes a new phase of faith a long time to get recognition at all, and still longer to work its adherents over, and entirely root out old prejudices, and clear away the obstructions to its work. The ground must be torn up, mountains leveled down or tunneled, valleys filled up, and much that looks like incendiary work done, before railroads can be built. When this work is going on, the question as to the good of railroads can not be answered by pointing to any particular good that one has done.

Notwithstanding Spiritualism is only beginning to get ready for operation, not being yet organized and harnessed into its work, I know of no Spiritualist who is not willing that the question of its *cui bono* shall now be submitted to the world, its works in every instance to furnish the answer.

I know of no better course to pursue in this investigation than that adopted by the Judean reformer. When John sent word, " Art thou he that should come, or do we look for another?" Jesus said to John's agents, " Go and show John again those things which ye do hear and see: The blind receive their sight, and the lame walk; the lepers are cleansed, and the deaf hear; the dead are raised up, and the poor have the gospel preached to them; and blessed is he whosoever shall not be offended in me." (Matt. xi. 3–6.)

Jesus intended that the divinity of his system of religion should be attested by its works. If his logic was good, the divinity of any religious system can be attested in the same way; if not, we still want proof that the world is better for having Christianity in it.

In speaking of agitators that were to come into the world, Jesus was very careful to instruct his pupils not to reject every new religious idea or teacher that should arise, — only the *false* ones were to be rejected; and the rule by which to try them was plain. His advice on the subject reads as follows: " Beware of false prophets, which come to you in sheep's clothing, but inwardly they are ravening wolves. Ye shall know them by their fruits. Do men gather grapes of thorns, or figs of thistles ? Even so every good tree bringeth forth good fruit; but a corrupt tree bringeth forth evil fruit. A good tree can not bring forth evil fruit, neither can a corrupt tree bring forth good fruit. Every tree that bringeth not forth good fruit is hewn down, and cast into the fire. Wherefore by their fruits ye shall know them." (Matt. vii. 15-20.)

That last sentence, " By their fruit ye shall know them," is right to the point. I wish people would abolish every rule of trying men or their religions, except by their fruit. That is as Jesus says: the way to try fruit trees, I care not how crooked, knotty, and scrubbed a fruit tree may be, if it bears an abundance of nice, luscious, healthy fruit, the farmer calls it a good tree, and takes care of it. Again, let the tree be ever so thrifty, straight, and grand, if it bears no fruit, or if its fruit is bitter or tasteless, — if its only production is thorns or thistles, it is pronounced a " corrupt tree," and cut down and burned. By this rule Spiritualists are willing their religion shall be tried. If Spiritualism has by this time produced no good fruit, though it is hardly old enough to be noticed as a tree at all, I am willing to help cut it down.

This, the only course of argument for me to pursue,

will make the case turn almost wholly on personal experiences; so permit me to record some experiences and some personal observations of the experience of others.

When Spiritualism came to me, it came with much such an announcement as it did to Saul of Tarsus: "I will show him how great things he must suffer for my name's sake." (Acts ix. 16.) Spiritualism faithfully warned me that it would yet deprive me of both friends and property. Could I at that time have taken the full meaning of that prophecy, I now think I should have looked back with no small amount of hankering for the "leeks and onions of Egypt;" but a partial unbelief was kindly vouchsafed me in this time of need. "But," added the good angel, "don't let this discourage you; new friends will soon gather around you, and your property will only be bread cast upon the waters,—you will gather it again."

Thus far the angels have been as good as their word. No sooner was I compelled by conviction to renounce the old and take hold of the new than every old-time friend was my enemy. Old friends went faster than new ones came. One misfortune followed another, until I found myself several hundred dollars in debt, and not a dollar to pay with. What was to be done? One Sunday morning, while residing in Milwaukee, my "cruse" not only scraped the bottom of the barrel, but it scraped when there was nothing there! There was a wife and four hungry children in the house, but not one bite of anything to eat, nor as much as five cents in money! Now I had come to my rope's end, what could I do? The children would soon be crying for bread, and no possibility of supplying, unless by begging or stealing. Kind reader, place yourself in that position, and many poor, who now rest under your censure, will instead receive your pity. It was at this time that I fully made up my mind — well, not exactly to renounce Spiritualism, for that can not be done, — but to renounce my work for the angels. I said, Spiritualism is true; but, *cui bono?* My spirit friends care nothing for me. I have given up all for them, — have served them faithfully ever since I knew of their existence, and yet they care nothing for me, — they would let me starve. To-morrow morning I will accept a situation offered me in the city, and let Spiritualists and Spiritualism take care of themselves. "No," said my best earthly friend, "you will not." I went to the post-office and found a letter, which I opened, and read as follows : —

"NEW YORK, August 6, 1866.

"MOSES HULL.

"My Dear Brother: I am impressed that you are in great need. Enclosed find my mite. I am very busy. Letters must be as brief as telegraphic despatches. Twenty thousand patients have been benefited by my magnetism since the first of May.

"Truly your brother,
"DR. J. R. NEWTON."

When I took the letter in my hand, for a few moments I did not stop to discuss the news contained in it. I was busy with another subject. Never, in my history, had ten dollars come so opportune, nor were words ever more fitly spoken. I reflected as follows: Who told the doctor that I had spent my last penny? How did he get the "impression" that I was in "great need?" What impulse was that? Why did it happen to move him at that time? Why was I selected as the subject? Why does this impression manifest such an intelligence and such an interest for me? Is not this the fulfillment of the promise made by my spirit friends, "Your bread and water shall be sure." I there and then resolved to trust the angels, and never, under any circumstances, renounce my allegiance to them. At that time the tide turned, and that which had flown from me began to flow back. I have ever been a poor, stubborn servant of the angels, — often a poor tool for them to use, — but have never, for one moment, felt to distrust them.

Now, permit me to invite attention to the news contained in the letter. "*Twenty thousand patients have been benefited by my magnetism since the first of May.*" Supposing Spiritualism never has done any good, excepting relieving pain. Again: supposing it never did any of that, except through the mediumship of Dr. Newton. Again: we will suppose they never used this one man only during the three months mentioned in this letter! Even then has not Spiritualism done some good in the world? Nay, have all the doctors in the city of New York done as much in any three months in their lives? Let me carry this argument further. You may throw off ninety per cent. of the number of cases that the doctor reported to have benefited by his magnetism during the three months mentioned in his letter, and then I submit that Spiritualism comes with *better* credentials from the angel-world than any other religion. Go to the poor sufferer, tortured with pain and scorched with fever, and ask him whether he could see the good of the power that would relieve him? And you have answered the question of the good of Spiritualism.

There I stopped writing long enough to glance at the Springfield Republican, just thrown into my door, and the first thing that met my eyes was so appropriate, that I yield to the impulse to copy it. Here it is:—

"THE SUICIDE OF AN AMERICAN GIRL IN LONDON occurred under very sad circumstances, about three weeks ago. She drowned herself at Waterloo Bridge, and the motives which impelled her to the act are vividly set forth in this letter, which she left behind her: The crime that I am about to commit, and what I suffer hereafter, is nothing compared to my present misery. Alone in London, not a penny, or a friend to advice or lend a helping hand, tired and weary with looking for something to do, failing in every way, footsore and heart-weary, I prefer death to the dawning of another wretched morning. I have only been in Britain nine weeks. I came as nursery-governess with a lady from America to Wick, in Scotland, where she discharged me, refusing to pay my passage back, giving me my wages, £3.10s. After my expenses to London, I found myself in this great city with only 5s. What was I to do? I sold my watch. The paltry sum I obtained for that soon went in paying for my board and in looking for a situation. Now I am destitute. Every day is a misery to me. No friend, no hope, no money: what is left? Oh, God of heaven, have mercy on a poor, helpless sinner; thou knowest how I have striven against this, but fate is against me. I can not tread the path of sin, for my dead mother will be watching me. Fatherless, motherless, home I have none. Oh, for the rarity of

Christian hearts. I am now mad; for days I have foreseen that this would be the end. May all who hear of my death forgive me, and may God Almighty do so, before whose bar I must soon appear. Farewell to all, to this beautiful and yet wretched world. ALICE BLANCHE OSWALD. I am twenty years of age the 14th of this month."

Was there ever anything more touching? "I can not tread the path of sin, for my dead mother will be watching me." How many thousands have been kept from sin by the same watchful care of those on the other side? How kind in that mother to tempt that poor, homeless, wandering, orphaned, outcast daughter over to the other side? There was not room for her in this world! No road open for her, except that of sin and shame. Let us rejoice that death's door ever stands ajar, and the deep waters always welcome such guests! What shall be said of the lady (?) who discharged the poor orphan girl in a strange country, without paying her enough, so that she could rereturn to her native land? Is there blood enough in all the animals of the Jewish system, or the saviors of all others, to atone for her heinous sins? One can but wish the poor unfortunate had given the name and address of the "lady from America." It would be well to know what church has the responsibility of the salvation of such a soul.

But I am ahead of my subject. Permit me now, under a distinct heading, to discuss the

TEMPORAL GOOD OF SPIRITUALISM.

Dr. J. G. Fish, in his debate with Mr. Dunn, in Rochester, N. Y., said, "Under the direction of his father — through Mr. Home as medium — the Czar of Russia liberated twenty millions of serfs. Abraham Lincoln, under the influence of his spiritual advisers, signed the Emancipation Proclamation at Washington."

The above is strictly true. Twenty-four millions of men and women, with their offspring, are to-day indebted to Spiritualism for their liberty. If liberty is a temporal blessing, Spiritualism has come laden with such.

The following I take from the same source. Mr. Beck, the gentleman with whom Lizzie Keizer resides, and Lizzie herself, have told me the same story. Those well acquainted with Miss Keizer, know many similar incidents in the history of her mediumship. I give it as related by Mr. Fish: —

"Lizzie Keizer, the medium, passing one day down the street, was accompanied by a person whom she supposed to be mortal. As they passed a building used for public purposes, the individual says to Lizzie, 'Look on the steps.' There sat an old man, care-worn, diseased, starving, and sick. The individual says, 'That is my father, but he can not see or hear me now.' 'Why,' said Lizzie, 'I thought you was in the body.' 'No, I am a spirit; that is my father; he wants to go to St. Louis, and wants money to buy bread.' Lizzie asked her name. 'My name is Elizabeth.' Lizzie went to the old man, and said, 'You are tired, sick, hungry, and want to go to St. Louis.' 'That is all true,' said the old man, 'but how did you know it?' Said Lizzie, 'Your daughter Elizabeth told me.' 'My daughter Elizabeth? Why, my daughter Elizabeth has been dead many years.' 'Yes,' said

Lizzie, 'I know that; but her spirit came along with me, and pointed you out to me, and told me all about it.' Tears rolled down the old man's cheek. He was destitute. The good girl gave him two dollars, *all she had in the world.* He went on his way. I wrote to the place where he went, and received a reply from the postmaster that he arrived safely, and died a few days after his arrival."

It was *five* dollars, and that of borrowed money, instead of two, that Lizzie gave the poor rheumatic sufferer. Probably the printers made the mistake in Mr. Fish's account of the matter. However, had it been only five cents, it was enough to help the old gentleman to his friends to die; and the test from his daughter Elizabeth afforded more pleasure than gold or silver could have purchased from the poor sufferer. Thousands of such incidents as these can be pointed out as a few of the good things resulting from communion with the world of angels.

A few personal experiences, under this heading, may not be inappropriate. After a somewhat extended investigation of the religions of different nations, including that of the Jews and Christians, I concluded that it had been an extensive, if not universal custom among ancient nations, for ministers or priests to be healers. So, to follow the example of the ancients, as well as benefit humanity, I concluded I would do the double work of preaching the gospel and healing the sick. This I followed more or less for several years, with a degree of success that would have warranted my continuing the same, could I, in justice to myself, have longer carried the double burden. In cases of healing by my own hands, if there were no other evidence of the good of the power which used me, I have found all I need on this part of the argument.

I have no authority to use names in the following case, yet I will furnish, for private use, names and address of witnesses, if wanted. At a hotel in a western city I was introduced to Col. ——, a gentleman who had no faith in Spiritualism; but as he had but little faith in other religions, and naturally inclined to investigate new things, he attended, and manifested a deep interest in my lectures. He came into my rooms several times during the week to talk over our philosophy. During one of his calls, something seemed to say to me, "You can cure his arm." I then noticed, for the first time, that his arm was useless, and apparently dead. Yet I could not pick up the courage to ask the unbelieving colonel to permit me to treat it. The next day he came to my rooms, and said, "I've come to test the virtue and power of your spirits. I have one of my awful headaches to-day. Nothing ever has cured my head when it commenced aching; it never quits until it gets its ache out." A moment convinced me that I could cure him. In five minutes more he was well. Then the impression came so strongly that I must work on that arm, that I could not resist the impulse to beg the privilege. "Certainly," was his reply; " but the arm is dead. You may as well go to the graveyard and try to manipulate a dead arm there to life. This arm has neither sense of feeling nor power of motion. It was shot with a poisoned arrow during the Indian war in Minnesota. It's a wonder I had not died. Everybody else beside me, that was wounded, died. In my case, only this arm died." Feeling a heavy influence upon me, I took hold of his withered, helpless hand. In a moment I felt a twitching in his fingers. In another moment the tips of his fingers were covered with perspiration. In thirty minutes he had the use of his hand and arm; and in an hour he was holding a composing-stick in that hand and setting type. This man had spent a small fortune in doctoring that hand, and received no benefit.

Now let us suppose there is nothing of Spiritualism except the healing of a few otherwise hopeless cases, similar to the one mentioned above, is not that enough of itself to answer the question as to whether any good is to result from the communion established between the two worlds?

In the village of Allegan, Mich., I once delivered one of my most earnest and violent lectures against Spiritualism. Fully believing Spiritualism to be immoral in its tendency, I never left an opportunity unimproved to warn the people against what I believed to be its delusive snares. At the conclusion of the lecture, a Spiritualist, with whom I had a passing acquaintance, asked me to hear his story, and, if possible, harmonize it with my theory. The following is the substance of what he related: —

"Not long since I attended a circle. After several interesting communications, a medium, in a deep trance, said to me, 'Go out on the street' (designating the place), 'and you will find a lady engaged in a low conversation with a man. She is needy; give her some money.' I went, and found the lady as directed, and handed her the amount of money I supposed she needed. As soon as she received the money, she said, 'Sir, you have saved me. This amount of money I must have had to-night, or my household goods would have been set in the street to-morrow morning. I could not pay my rent. I was never used to doing business before my husband was killed in the war. Now I am alone in the world, and have the care of four helpless children. I have tried every honorable means of obtaining a livelihood, and failed. I have labored and prayed earnestly for some way to open by which I could make an honest living; and now, as a last resort, I had proposals, and would have been compelled to sell my virtue for money to buy bread for my children and pay my rent.' Now, said he, if Spiritualism is evil, and all evil, as you represent, how do you account for this, and a thousand similar cases?"

Sure enough, a few such cases are worth more to determine the effects of Spiritualism than all the theories in the world. I do not relate this to show the moral effect of Spiritualism, as illustrated in the salvation of the lady's virtue, for it did not save her virtue. I do not regard a lady as having lost her virtue because external circumstances *compel* her to sell herself to save her children from the poorhouse, any more, nor as much, as I regard the lady who marries for a home and position in society as being a prostitute. The salvation in this case consisted, at least in part, of a *temporal* blessing, — the relief of her immediate wants. In addition to that, she saved herself the humiliation of being compelled to surrender her ladyhood for a living.

The Spiritualists of America are aware that the firm of William White & Co., of the city of Boston, every week of the world dispense spiritual light and food to the multitude through their widely-circulated Banner of Light. They may not all be aware that there is connected with this publishing-house what they call a "bread-fund;" that the poor can go there at any time and get tickets for enough bread to supply their immediate necessities. But I often wonder whether the hundreds of persons who have been supplied with bread from this source, that otherwise must have suffered, know that they are directly indebted to the spirit-world for that supply? That "bread-fund" originated in the spirit-world. The necessity of such a fund, and method of operating it, was suggested by a departed human spirit, through the mediumship of Mrs. Conant. Probably one half of the money that has been contributed to sustain it has been given under the direct influence, or at the earnest request of departed human spirits. Does this look as though Spiritualism had come to do any good?

I know a medium who owes his life to the fact, that the spirits took him by force out of a railroad car, and off of the train at the last station, before it collided with another, killing several passengers, among whom was the one occupying the seat he vacated. Could all the passengers have been under the influence of such wise and tender guides they might all have been saved. Could engineers and conductors all come under such power, what a world of accidents could be prevented! This alone would make Spiritualism worth more than all the religions of the world. Many such cases have occurred.

A mediumistic engineer, near Eyota, Minn., saw the familiar form of an old lady jump on to his train in the night. She stood and looked at him for a moment, and said, "For God's sake, stop your train!" He immediately whistled "down brakes," and got his train stopped within about four feet of where the track was torn up. He learned the next day that the old lady had been in the spirit world only about an hour when this occurred.

When Peter West, a noted medium from Chicago, was returning home from the army, he run out of money, and got the privilege of firing from Albany to Buffalo. He had never been over the route before. Suddenly a spirit came to him, and said, "The bridge just around the curve is broken." He said to the engineer, "Is there not a bridge just ahead?" On being answered that there was, he said, "There is a spirit here that tells me to have you stop the train, as the bridge is broken down." The train was stopped, and scores of lives saved. The railroad officers were so grateful that they furnished a pass, sending the poor medium to Chicago, and the passengers attested their gratitude by presenting him a purse of money.

An engineer on the P. Ft. W. & C. R. W., by the name of Aimes, a personal acquaintance of the writer, stopped and switched his train at Hobart, Ind., in obedience to a spirit command, just in time to save a collision with a late train from Chicago.

Father Lindsley, at Rural, Ohio, started to meeting one night, but was commanded by spirits to go back, as his house was on fire. He turned, and hastened home, just as the flames were bursting up from coals that had fallen on the floor. He saved his house by spirit direction.

An entranced medium, in the city of Worcester, Mass., handed me two dollars, stating that I would meet a barefooted little girl, and I might get her a pair of shoes with it. The same evening, the 8th of March, 1864, I met a little barefooted beggar girl in the city of Lynn, who said, "Please sir, give me five cents to buy a candle with; my pa is dead, and my ma is sick, and we have no milk for the babe." I opened my pocket-book to give the child five cents, when I noticed that two-dollar bill lying by itself; it brought the spirit message to my mind. I then noticed that the child was barefooted, although it was snowing. I handed her, in addition to the five cents with which to buy a candle, the two-dollar bill. Said she, "Are you going to give me all of this?" "Yes," said I; "it is all yours." "Oh, goodie, goodie, goodie!" said she, "I have enough to buy a pair of shoes." Reader, that little girl, for the first time in many months, was happy then; and I never felt so well over an agency in my life, as in the fact, that I had been the agent to carry that two dollars to that little girl. Does Spiritualism come with temporal blessings in its hands?

I personally know of more than a dozen useful inventions, given by the spirits, that have been patented. The artesian well of Chicago, and more than a score of oil wells in Pennsylvania, were located by spirits. Lost wills, deeds, property, and people have been found, and stolen money discovered and recovered by spirits; and yet people say, *cui bono?*

Permit me now to enter upon the investigation of the

MORAL GOOD

resulting from Spiritualism. For the argumentative part of this division of the subject, I will refer the reader to a former volume,* and to former parts of this work. I will here only relate a short dialogue, and a few incidents.

Not long since, a gentleman in one of Indiana's leading towns, who had recently renounced Methodism, and taken hold of Spiritualism, asked me to go and spend the night with him. Said he, "I don't know how my wife will treat you; she is very bitter in her opposition to Spiritualism, but has consented to have you spend a night and a day in our house. I hope you will do her some good."

I found the lady, as announced by her husband, very bitter in her opposition, and violent in her language. I tried to reason with her that night and the next morning, but to no purpose. After her husband had gone to his work, she came into my room, bathed in tears, and said, "Mr. Hull, please do not lead my husband further on the road to ruin. Only just think; one year since, he was a respectable man, and a class-leader in the Methodist church!" Said I, "You must not think Spiritualism is leading everybody to hell, because your husband has become a bad man from his connection with it. Evil will work out; and your husband's evil would have come to light in some other way if he had not become a Spiritualist." Our dialogue then assumed about the following form: —

* Question Settled, pp. 40-45, published by William White & Co., Boston. Price $1.50. Postage 16 cents.

Lady. My husband's *evil*, did you say? Sir, I want you to understand that he is not a bad man.

Hull. Oh, I misunderstood you! I had supposed, from what I had learned in the village, that he was a good man; but your representations had changed my mind. You tell of the high and respectable position from which he has fallen: I inferred that Spiritualism had made him bad.

Lady. In a certain sense it has; but then he does not do any really criminal things.

Hull. He is not so good a husband as he was when he became a Spiritualist, is he?

Lady. Well, if it is any of your business, he is as good. There never was a better husband in the world than mine.

Hull. But is he a good father? Does he provide well for his children? Does he treat them well?

Lady. Why, his children are seemingly his idols; no father could treat his children better than he treats his. If anything, he is not so rigid with them as when he belonged to the church.

Hull. I am really glad he is as good a husband and father as in his Christian days; there are, according to that, two relations in which Spiritualism has not spoiled him. The fact of his not being so good a neighbor as in former times, may be accounted for on the ground that the prejudice of his neighbors against Spiritualism may have caused them to treat him differently from what they did before his change of sentiment.

Lady. But he is as good a neighbor as he ever was. Spiritualism has not injured him in the least in that respect.

Hull. It has not? Well, if Spiritualism has not injured him as a husband, father, or neighbor, please tell me what injury it has done him? Is he not as good a Christian as ever?

Lady. So far as doing his duty by everybody and thing by which he is surrounded is concerned, he is; otherwise he is not.

Hull. In what sense is he not a Christian?

Lady. Why, he would prefer to spend his Sundays in the fields, or woods, or reading old Davis's books, or, sometimes I think even fishing or hunting, rather than going to the church, where in former days he took such delight.

Hull. I see the point. He prefers to go into God's great library and read the bibles God printed on all nature, to reading a man-made book, that you call the Bible. He prefers to read the writings of A. J. Davis, rather than to attend the church. His crime is against the Methodist ministry and church. That is unpardonable. Now, if you will show me that he has sinned against God or nature, I will try to point out to him the error of his ways.

Lady. I do not claim that he is a great sinner; I only claim that I don't want Spiritualism to ruin my family.

Hull. Is your family on the verge of ruin? I am sorry.

Lady. O, I don't know as it is; but I did tell him, when he began to attend circles and talk about Spiritualism, that I would not live with him if he embraced it.

Hull. That is the way Spiritualism ruins families. One party embraces it, and the other says, I won't live with you unless I can dictate you in matters of religious opinion. Now he does not object to your being a Methodist: if you will be as liberal as he, all will be well. When I commenced this conversation, I expected to find your husband a bad man; instead, I find you a very illiberal, sectarian woman, chagrined because he will not permit you to take charge of his conscience. Permit me to say here, that in every case where I have attempted to investigate the evils of Spiritualism, I have, instead of finding it evil, found a petty tyrant trying to dictate a course of life to another. You have no more right to dictate your husband's faith to him, or call him a bad man because he will not throw away his judgment for yours, than you have to dictate when and what he shall eat or drink, or when he shall rest or sleep.

Suffice it to say that this conversation put her on a new train of thought, which culminated in her investigating her husband's character from a different standpoint; also, in her indorsing the very reading and preaching that she condemned her husband for studying, including even what she had designated as ." Old Davis's works." In a majority of cases where we hear charges of the immoral tendency of Spiritualism, an investigation brings the same result.

Not many years since I had a talk with the president of a Spiritualist society in one of our principal cities. I spoke of my full belief that the tendency of Spiritualism was toward, and not from, morality. He said, " I am a partial illustration of what Spiritualism can do; I tell you, because you can use it for the benefit of others and the advancement of the cause. I inherited from my father an appetite for intoxicating drink. I was drunk before I was six years old, and every opportunity between that and the time I was thirty-six. I never paid any attention to Spiritualism, or thought anything of it, but effectually tried the other religions, and the doctors, and about everything else of the age, to cure me of my ungovernable appetite for intoxicating liquors. All proved of no effect; my money, the use of my brains, my happiness, and that of my family, were all exhausted. I would have traded my last pair of boots for soul and body poisoning alcohol.

"I was in this condition when a series of Spiritual meetings were being conducted in this city. The lecturer, one of the most popular lady lecturers we ever had, on returning home from meeting on Sunday, received a request from one of her spirit guides to go into a drinking saloon and take me out. My mother had requested this spirit to do this work. Though her friends, many of them leading Spiritualists, protested against this act, she went into the saloon, found me, more than half drunk, and though I was an entire stranger to her she took me home, preached to me, magnetized me, put me under spirit power, and took from me that inherited appetite for intoxicating liquors. Though that was near seven years since, from that day to this no intoxicating drink of any kind has ever touched my lips."

This man lived six years longer, a sober, honest, industrious, and with the exception of his Spiritualism, a *respectable* man. As long as he could speak his lips praised the religion that had prepared him for the better world. Among his last requests was the one that a Spiritualist should preach at his funeral, and use the victories he had obtained as an evidence of the good of getting in communication with our ascended brethren. This case is only a sample. There are hundreds like it in many particulars. Say, do such things prove Spiritualism to be a temporal and moral blessing? The name of the individual above mentioned, and the names and addresses of witnesses can be given by application to the author of this volume.

I personally know of several other cases of a similar kind. An old man in Wisconsin was saved, and effectually cured of the habit of intoxication by his son, who had been killed in the army, appearing from time to time to him in the drinking saloon, entreating him not to drink, sometimes knocking a well-filled glass out of his hand, and finally bringing him under an influence by which he controlled his appetite. A man in Chicago was saved in the same way by the return of a spirit daughter who gave him a prescription, the use of which cured him of the disease called "common drunkard." Only this morning an incident was related to me, by a responsible party, of an inveterate chewer and smoker of tobacco, being saved from that useless and filthy habit by the spirits causing tobacco to make him sick. This was the last resort: all other means had failed.

A man who is now one of our best Spiritualistic writers, thirty years since, when a respectable member of a church, paid his fare on a steamboat; the clerk, by mistake, handed him in change two five-dollar bills instead of one. His first thought was, I will return the extra bill; after that he reflected that the steamboat company was rich and he was poor; he would keep the bill; the company would never miss it, and certainly there could be no harm in his taking the advantage of that circumstance. Thus his conscience was eased, and he kept the money near twenty years, until he became a medium. As soon as he came *en rapport* with the spirit world, he was told of that stain on his soul, and no rest was given him, day or night, until he went to the company and paid them that money with the interest. No atonement — nothing but integrity, *strict, unswerving fidelity to justice*, could avail in his case. If every pretended Christian in the world could to-day exchange his imputed righteousness for such an influence, the world would stand morally higher than it does. Why should not Spiritualism lead to a higher and purer life? It ever approaches man's best faculties, always appealing to the very highest social qualities of his nature. Even admitting that your very best friends in the spirit world are not with you, the *thought* entertained by Spiritualists that they are, will have much the same effect as though they were present. Spiritualists generally believe that their spirit friends are with them, watching and guarding, pleased with their efforts to rise in the scale of purity, and grieved with their violations of the principles of rectitude — that their most secret thoughts are read by their spirit friends as readily as an expert would read an open book. This is not all: the commission of sin envelopes the sinner in an atmosphere of sin that can be seen, tasted, and *felt* by every sensitive medium with whom he comes in contact.

Spiritualists do not believe that there are or can be any secrets. They believe that every stone, to the one who can read, tells how it was made; that every tree of the forest tells of every dry or wet season through which it passed; that knots and scars tell to the reader, of accidents which occurred a century since; so they claim that even your *sins* will find you out. It will be impossible to flee from either your sins or their scars. This world and the other will read them all; that the final and total consequence of sin must fall upon the one who commits it; nothing can step in between the act and the actor. Believing this, will they not be more inclined to try to live stainless lives? I believe the history of Spiritualists and Spiritualism will, when fairly written, show such to be the fact. The thought of being surrounded by the pure and good, must lead to thoughts and acts of the same kind.

> "With a slow and noiseless footstep
> Come the messengers divine,
> Take the vacant chair beside me,
> Lay their gentle hands in mine.
>
> "And they sit and gaze upon me,
> With those deep and tender eyes,
> Like the stars, so still, and saint-like,
> Looking downward from the skies.
>
> "Uttered not, yet comprehended,
> Is the spirit's voiceless prayer
> Soft wishes in blessings ended,
> Breathing from their lips of air."

THE MENTAL GOOD

Growing out of Spiritualism can not, in this short chapter, be told. It has, in almost every case, developed and quickened the mental powers of its mediums, not only so, but its soothing power is beyond computation. Among the instances of the mental soothing effects of Spiritualism only two will be told. The first I give in substance as related to me by witnesses, the second came under my own observation.

A young man in Chicago persuaded his widowed mother to let him go to the war. When she gave her consent, she urged upon him the immediate necessity of embracing Christ, as his new perils would render his life more precarious and uncertain than ever before. His response was, "Mother, I would if but for your sake if I could, but as I have often told you, I am unfortunate in my organization; I can not believe in your religion." Thus he went to the war an unregenerated infidel. He fell in his first engagement with the enemy. When the telegraph flashed the news back to the old Christian lady, that her son was killed, she exclaimed, "*My boy is in hell!* He did not believe in Christ; he was a good boy but not a Christian: I must go to hell with my child; I could not leave him in that horrid place alone. No, a mother's love will follow her son there; I will go with my child."

Her minister told her that her son was a good boy, and tried to persuade her that he was not in hell. He had died in his country's cause. In an hour of peril like this, the cause of the country was next to the cause of Christ; there was hope for her son. All this argument was wasted on the old lady; she had drank deeply of the doctrines of the church. She argued logically, too; that her son had died out of Christ, and hence exposed to hell. The church had no consolation for her; she became partially insane, and it was only by the most vigilant and patient watchfulness that she was kept from committing suicide, in order, as she said, to join her boy in hell. At last, after a great deal of persuading, she was induced to visit a test medium. Soon her son came, but unable to control much, gave place to his father, who related the circumstances of the boy's death, and told of his condition in the spirit world, giving her new light with regard to both hell and heaven. This interesting seance was concluded by inviting the old lady to visit another medium, giving the name and place, and informing her that it was probable that her son could control the medium. The taste she had got was enough to cause the old lady to long for more. She visited the other medium, and got tests from her own dear boy. This of course was followed by other manifestations, resulting in her complete emancipation from the church and its dogmas. The result was, she became calm and even happy. Her mind was restored to its balance, and the lunatic asylum cheated out of a victim.

Was this good? Every other help had been sought, and failed. No arm was found strong enough to rescue this old lady, except Spiritualism. There are thousands in the asylums to-day who have gone there from similar causes to that which come so near sending this old lady into a lunatic's cell. Let us extol the religion that would make even insane retreats houses of praise.

The only remaining incident to which I would refer, happened in Iowa. An ordinarily good man, in the heat of political controversy, became offended at something said, and swore he would have the life of the offender. During a fit of insanity, caused by intoxication, he undertook to execute his threat, and lost his life in the attempt. The man's brother, who was a minister, said, "My brother was a wicked man. He was a drunkard, and died with murder in his heart. My brother is in hell; I know he is." He went to the newly-made widow, even while her husband's corpse was yet in the house, and said, "I would not have a funeral sermon; no minister can do his duty without telling you your husband is suffering the eternal burnings." The lady became distracted, and at times perfectly insane. The church had no consolation for her; even the Universalists could not console her; their theories seemed so much like hypotheses that their words had no effect. About sixteen miles from where this happened there lived a medium. Suddenly an irresistible influence came to him, and he ran as straight as a bee-line to the widow; he jumped fences and walls, ran through swamps and creeks, and scaled steep hills, letting nothing swerve him from his course, or purpose after he got there. When he reached the lady's house he demanded to see her; and though all regarded him as crazy, he was granted a private interview. What he said or did is not definitely known to outsiders, but one thing is known: the distracted lady became calm and cheerful; she said she had heard from her husband; that he was working out his own salvation on the other side, as he would have been compelled to have done on this, had he staid here. She found in the spirit world itself the consolation which could not be furnished by any of the religions by which she was surrounded.

I have now gone through an entire chapter, picking up here a grain and there a grain of good that has come from Spiritualism. I would not represent this as the harvest of good to be reaped, as the result of the new religion. These are a few of the *specimens* only which have been gathered from " wayside gleanings." The great Spiritual mines are filled with such and better. "Eye hath not seen, ear hath not heard, neither hath it entered into the heart of man to conceive the things Spiritualism has provided for the world."

The great boon of all, the one needed when no other can reach the case, is the consolation it affords to those about to exchange worlds. The fear of death is gone! The fires of hell have been extinguished! The walls are taken down from the celestial city! The ivory or golden throne is removed, and flowers planted on the spot it occupied! Its God is not a tyranical king, with a crown upon his head and a scowl on his face, but a loving father and mother ever looking after the welfare and comfort of all the children! The dying Spiritualist knows he is not to be forced millions of miles away from those in whom he has an interest; he is not going away, but remains to bless and be blessed by those yet on earth's side of death's river. O, may the blessed consolations of Spiritualism cheer both reader and writer in the hour of dissolution!

CHAPTER VI.

MINOR QUESTIONS.

Asking and answering Questions, the difference. — Can not answer every Question. — Spiritualism necessarily crude at first. — May be modified. — How do Spirits operate? — Their Power over the Will. — Does Mediumship indicate a weak Mind. — The controlling Spirit not necessarily with the Medium. — Author's Experiments. — Spirits control more than One at a time. — Sometimes control without knowing it. — A. J. Davis and Professor Vaughan. — "Arabula" and "Human Nature." — E. D. Keene gives a Communication from a Man yet on Earth. — Why do Spirits lie? — Fault often in the Medium. — Psychological Experiments. — Cause of Failure. — Reason why some get better Tests than others. — Why do not all Mediums give Tests. — Tests not always from personal Friends. — Psychology and Spiritualism. — All are Mediums. — David and his Mediums. — Philosophy of Dark Circles. — Biblical Manifestations in the Dark. — The Explanation. — Morality of Spiritualism. — Mediumship a Quickener. — Spiritualism and Sunshine. — Webster, Clay, et al., whittled down. — The Explanation. — How to receive Spiritualism. — Why so many Indian Spirits. — The Indian Element positive. — Belongs in this Country. — Better Magnetizers. — More easily imitated Humbugs and the Self-deceived. — Experience of the Author. — Where are the Ancients. — Reasons why they do not return. — What Good can Spiritualism do? — For what should we go to Spirits. — Demonstrates a Future. — What will Science do? — Spiritual Sense. — Immortality Triumphant.

THIS chapter I design as an answer to the ever recurring questions concerning the *modus operandi* of many of the spirit manifestations. Nearly everything that I shall say here will be said by the request of individuals who have handed in questions which they wished answered in the present volume.

Asking questions is an easy matter. Answering them is sometimes a hard one. Questions are generally based on the ignorance of the one who asks;

answers, if correct, are always based on the knowledge of the one answering; and as there is so much more that we do not know than that we do know, it can not be expected that any one can throw all the light on any department of any subject that can be desired. I have classified the questions received during the last few months, and propose to answer such, and only such, as seem to have been asked in a spirit of candid inquiry. Those asked for strife and illegitimate contention will not be noticed.

It can not be expected that in a book of no greater dimensions than I design to make this, written to elicit the attention of those who would not touch a heavier volume, every objection can be met, and every question answered. I do not design to do that, yet there are hundreds of honest people in the world, who only need an explanation of a few "whys" and "wherefores," to enable them to see the most perfect harmony between the philosophy and phenomena of modern Spiritualism. For the benefit of such this chapter is written.

Every theory of philosophy or religion is necessarily crude and undigested at the first; but potent and persevering investigation will lead to the discovery of truth. If Spiritualists, as they are led to more thoroughly and critically examine their system, should in many instances be induced to modify it somewhat, it would be no more than others have done. My hope is that Spiritualists will be more swift to re-shape, re-mold, re-make, or retract extravagant views, than have been their orthodox neighbors. It is much better to turn a coat, which in haste was put on wrong, than to obstinately refuse to adjust a garment because your friend, or even an enemy discovered the mistake before it was discovered by yourself; so, if, in answering questions, I should prune Spiritualism of some of its excrescences, let no Spiritualist tremble lest I should fell the tree. Spiritualism has a strong hold of life, and can endure harder thrusts than my poor pen could give it if I were disposed to write it down. I only intend to cut away a few of the thorns and thistles, so that the spiritual tree can live a tamer, sweeter life, and bear " much fruit." The deliciousness of which certainly would be marred if the work were left undone. " What is the chaff to the wheat, saith the Lord."

QUERY NO. 1.

How do spirits get into media, and what becomes of the medium spirit while the organism is being controlled by another?

Answer. It has been supposed that spirits control by getting into the physical system of the medium. Even Bible Spiritualists supposed that spirits entered into media. Ezekiel says, several times, that "The spirit entered into me." Mediums and spirits often speak in the same way. The trut' is, spirits can, and often do, as I will demonstrate, control, without knowing how they do it. The idea of spirits entering into the mediums is a mistake. Spirits do not enter into the media, but control them by coming into psychological *rapport* with them, as the psychologist controls his subject. A psychologist enters into his subject in every sense of the word that a spirit does into his. They each control by will power alone; the will, the mind, and spirit of the subject become negative, and yield to the positive power of the operator. The voluntary organs of every living creature are controlled by the creature; so when the operator gets control of the *will* of the subject, he, through that will, controls the physical organism. He may thus, when the control is perfect, enable the subject to speak any language he himself understands, or tell anything which he himself could tell. This control of a subject by an operator in the form, is *real* and *spiritual*, as much as any spirit control; the only difference being that one operator is clothed in flesh and blood, and the other is not.

QUERY NO. 2.

In that case is it not the weaker mind that is controlled by the stronger?

Answer. No; not necessarily. There is a difference between strength of mind and strength of will. A weak mind may accompany a strong will, and a strong mind a weak will; but neither the mind nor the *will* of the medium is necessarily weak. Mediumship implies the power to hold still and catch the positive influence that may be at work; " only this and nothing more." A state of sound sleep is as strong evidence of a weak mind, or weak will, as can be found in mediumship. Mediumship signifies the power to become passive, negative, quiet. Strong minds may sometimes pass into that condition more readily than weak ones; yet as strong minds are more liable to be positively engaged in some positive work, they may not always be so receptive as minds not so active. Large spirituality, with a disposition to approach the intellectual through the intuitional, rather than the spiritual through the intellectual, would perhaps render a person a better subject for influences.

QUERY NO. 3.

Are spirits necessarily present when they control mediums?

Answer. I think I have proof that they are not always within a few feet of the one controlled. I am personally acquainted with the fact of a spirit going into a circle, and through a medium who knew nothing of the subject of astronomy, giving a very interesting lecture on that subject. The same night, at the same hour, the same spirit purported to control another medium more than two hundred miles distant, and gave the same lecture. It might here be added, that this spirit had controlled each of these mediums on former occasions. I have myself, after psychologically controlling subjects, exercised a positive control over them when they were many miles away. I have made two mediums at the same time dream out the description of the scenery on the Hudson River as it passed before my eyes, as I passed up the river on a beautiful moonlight night, neither of the mediums at the time being within three hundred miles. These thoughts of course suggest

QUERY NO. 4.

Can spirits control more than one medium at a time?

Answer. Yes, most emphatically. Who has not seen speakers control whole audiences? Go to any protracted revival meeting, when in the height of its glory, and see how the audience can be swayed by its leader or leaders. This control is spiritual, and yet is often effected not only without the operator's having a knowledge of the *modus operandi*, but in many cases without his even having a knowledge of the fact of his control over the audience.

Many suppose they know a good deal of Spiritualism; but the truth is we are as yet hardly into its alphabet. I am convinced that spirits often control, and enable mediums to deliver eloquent discourses, without even themselves knowing they are exercising any control over the mediums. I have several times, when I have been thinking on a particular theme, met friends who, after exchanging a few preliminary compliments, would of their own accord enter into conversation, taking up the very thread of my thoughts, and in a few instances, upon questioning the parties, I learned that they never before entered into a conversation on that particular subject. What was this but a positive influence passing from mind to mind, which, if I had been out of the body, might have been called a spirit communication.

Several peculiar circumstances now occur to my mind, which will serve to throw light on some of the laws governing mediumship.

1. It will be remembered that A. J. Davis once gave the world some thoughts which were handed him from the higher spheres, on the philosophy of rain and the manner of producing it. About the same time Professor Vaughan came out with a lecture on the same subject, embodying the same ideas. Mr. Davis was accused of plagiarism. I fully believe that Mr. Davis was in this and all other instances honest, and that his thoughts came as he reported. Yet I can not see why the lecture may not have originated with Professor Vaughan. Why not? The positive

thoughts originated in Mr. Vaughan's brain, or passing through it from a higher source, reached Mr. Davis, and he was sufficiently negative to catch them, and fasten them on paper. The medium attracts the thoughts sent out by positive minds, in many instances without the sender knowing it. As the earth to-night drinks the rain which falls upon it, so very many mediums are sponges which absorb and give out again the thought that comes in their reach.

2. Not many years since " Arabula," a book of great merit, was produced through the mediumship of A. J. Davis, but the readers of " Human Nature," a magazine published in London, know that at the same time *the same thought*, and *sometimes the same words*, for page after page, were being published in Europe. The magazine above referred to, in the year 1868, I think it was, placed many paragraphs from the two works in juxtaposition, thus illustrating that they were essentially the same. Now, who plagiarized? I answer, no one. The thoughts which some one, who was sufficiently sensitive, caught as they passed through the old world, were caught by Mr. Davis when they came here, and perhaps in neither instance did the one who gave off these thoughts realize that they were contagious, or knew anything about these men catching them. If this idea should prove to be a truth (and it will), will we not all try to be more careful even of our secret thoughts, for they go out as positive entities, to work on the sensitives or mediums.

3. I have never met a better test medium than Edwin D. Keene, of Philadelphia; but in giving tests in the city of Washington, in April, 1870, this medi--

um said, "There is a spirit here who says his name is —— [The names I do not remember.] He wishes to talk to ——. He says he wronged you once; he feels badly about it, and that he can not progress until he confesses it, and obtains your forgiveness." He then proceeded to give the particulars of their difficulty, containing several remarkable tests, after which he again asked forgiveness for the great wrong he had done. The man, after telling the spirit that he was forgiven, responded that all was true, but he did not know that —— was dead; the last known of him was that he lived in Providence, R. I. A telegram was sent to Providence the next day, and the facts were all found to be true, *except that the man was at that time alive and well.* Now, how is this? I know of no explanation only that the medium came *en rapport* with the *acts* and *thoughts* of that individual; these acts and thoughts representing themselves as positive entities. If this is the true philosophy of mediumship, a spirit can as easily influence a dozen at a time as one. The power is not so much in spirit, as in the number of receptive individuals who come into his sphere. Who has not seen psychologists influence a dozen at a time, — sometimes making one believe that he was a minister, another that he was a desperate sinner, who needed salvation, and so on almost *ad infinitum?*

QUERY NO. 4.

Why do spirits so often tell that which is not true?

Answer. I doubt whether spirits often indulge in telling willful falsehoods. The communications proving to be false are usually either deceptions on the part of the medium, a reflection from the mind of those to whom the communication is made, or the result of an imperfect control. The best that can be done, a spirit can not always make a medium speak the truth. During the last half score of years I have had a very extended experience as a psychological operator, which has enabled me to look with more charity on the false in phenomenal Spiritualism than in former days. I have learned that, do the best I can, it is impossible to find a medium that can always be made to speak the truth. They can often be made to talk eloquently, and sometimes logically, but no one can be made to always talk truthfully. Let one case suffice as an illustration. As I have not the privilege of using names, allow me to supply their place with blanks. At a large dinner party in an eastern city, I once introduced a conversation on the wonders of psychology, when I was requested to produce some experiments. There was present in the room a Miss D., whom I had previously put under psychological control, and found as good as any subject I had ever seen. After obtaining her consent she was placed *en rapport* with my own spirit, and then requested to give tests of various kinds, which she did with astonishing success. She was thoroughly blindfolded, and in that condition could read any sentence brought before my eyes, tell anything I could have told, and even at our request look through solid walls, and tell what was going on in other rooms of the house. Finally the lady of the house led her to the pictures on the wall, and notwithstanding her eyes were closely bandaged, she correctly described every one, and told who every painting or photograph was made to represent. But this state of things was not to continue. While in the height of our success, she was led to a large portrait of a former husband of the lady who led her. "Who is that?" said the lady. "That is your brother," responded the clairvoyant. "A mistake," said the lady; "look again." After a moment's hesitation and a little closer observation, she responded, "It is your brother." All this time I used all of my will power to make her say husband. Finally I spoke in a positive tone of voice, and said, "Miss D., that is Mrs. H.'s husband." "Why," said she, "is not Mr. H. her husband?" "Yes," I responded; "but this is the first husband, who is now in the world of spirits."

"Well," said she, "the first thought came husband; but when I saw Mr. H. standing by my side, I could not say husband, I was compelled to say brother."

Now, what was this? I supposed the medium to be entirely unconscious; but the facts were, that some latent power of her brain was all the time reasoning on the impossibility of the lady having two husbands, and the idea of a very near relative was thrown on the mind, and hence she said, brother. Now, had I been in the spirit world, and influenced that medium as I did, she would probably have made the same mistake, and then I, as a spirit, would have been accused of lying, when in reality it would have been impossible for me to have made my medium tell the truth. The laws controlling mediumship are very subtle, and as yet only partially understood. A more thorough understanding of them may teach us to be cautious about accusing our risen friends of deliberately telling that which is not true.

While spirits control media by will power alone, we should not be astonished if the will of those forming the circle may partially spoil an otherwise good and true communication. One thing has been noticed, that is, that some persons get more truthful communications than others. The reason of this is, their mind or will is in a condition to permit spirits to more properly represent themselves than they can do in the presence of others.

QUERY NO. 8.

Why can not all mediums give names, dates, and other tests?

Answer. Spirits have ever been more ready in answering questions of a philosophic character than those of a test nature. The reason I understand to be this. Questions of a philosophic nature are usually out of the reach of the mediums, hence their mind can not so easily become active on them, as on questions containing tests. When a test question is asked, many mediums instantly fear they will fail to answer. This fear renders them so positive that the spirit can not approach them with the answer. I am not one who believes that every one in the spirit world can return and communicate. I doubt whether all or half that have gone to the spirit world can manifest through media at all. I do not believe that one test spirit manifestation in twenty comes directly from the spirit giving the test. I know that no more than one in twenty whom we meet in every-day life would succeed as practical psychologists; it is reasonable to suppose that those who could not psychologize a person in earth life, would not do it in spirit life. Of course this suggests the query, How do the spirit manifestations come? I answer, I have many times seen persons put under psychologic control, and then the operator put *en rapport* with persons in the room, who, under ordinary circumstances could not have controlled the subject. Yet all the while the operator kept supreme control, and others were by *his* will brought into and driven out of communication with the subject. So in spirit control. Each medium is surrounded with his or her spirit guides, who may, for the benefit of friends on either side of the river of death, serve in connection with the medium, as a connecting link between the two parties. Now take into consideration the peculiarities of the medium, then the peculiarities of the control by which he may be surrounded, and that all these peculiarities must in cases of test be overcome, and any one can see how difficult it may be to always give tests, and yet how easy it may be to give discourses where the power controlling has only his own thoughts to utter.

QUERY NO. 9.

Why can not all be mediums and see spirits?

Answer. There is a sense in which all are mediums. Paul says, " But the manifestation of the spirit is given to every man to profit withal." (1 Cor. xii. 7.) Every one who has a spirit, has something that can come *en rapport* with spirit. Hence all are mediums, though all may not have that one gift of seeing. In Paul's enumeration of the gifts, in the above mentioned chapter, he has them as follows: —

1. The Word of Wisdom.
2. The Word of Knowledge.

3. Faith
4. The gifts of healing.
5. The working of miracles.
6. Prophecy.
7. Discerning of spirits.
8. Diverse kinds of tongues.
9. Interpretation of tongues.

There are very few but that have, or could have, some of these or some other gifts. All can, by complying with proper conditions, be mediums.

As to seeing spirits, it requires a peculiar kind of mediumship to enable a person to see them either clairvoyantly or psychologically. These are the only ways persons as mediums can see spirits. Spirits sometimes, in the presence of certain organisms, gather a body from elements there are in the room; then all can see them without the aid of mediumship.

A clairvoyant sees spirits by means of having his spiritual eyes opened. A psychological subject sees them by passing *en rapport* with some power who wills him or her to see them. Mediumship, for extraordinary manifestations, has always been withheld from the masses of mankind. David was a smart man and good poet, yet, when he wished to "inquire of the Lord," he did not use his own mediumship, but sent for Nathan the prophet, or Gad the seer. Thus all could not be mediums, even for the Hebrew God.

Balaam could not see the angel that was plainly visible to the animal on which he rode. Elisha's servant could not see the hosts of angels by which he was surrounded until Elisha had put his hands on his head. It is no more strange that all can not be clairvoyants, than it is that all cannot be poets or orators.

The Longfellows, Whittiers, Patrick Henrys, and Wendell Phillipses are about as scarce as the Swedenborgs and A. J. Davises.

QUERY NO. 10.

Why is darkness required for certain forms of manifestation?

Answer. Before entering upon a direct reply to the above, permit me to ask a few questions. Why were the great Biblical manifestations nearly all performed in the dark? Even when heaven and earth were created, it was in the dark; "and darkness brooded on the face of the deep." (Gen. i. 1-2.) The Bible God "dwells in the midst of thick darkness." (1 Kings viii. 12.) When God threw Jacob in his wrestling-match it was in the dark. As soon as it began to be light, he pleaded, "let me go, for the day breaketh." (Gen. xxxii. 24.) The miracle of pulling Pharaoh's linchpins out was done in the dark. (Ex. xiv. 20-30.) Jesus' resurrection, the greatest of miracles, occurred in the night, so that he appeared to the woman before daylight. (John xx. 1.)

All who have investigated the subject tell us that darkness is a negative condition of the elements. The reason spirits can not speak to us in the light as well as in the dark is, they can not speak to our physical ears without forming physical organs of speech; these organs are organized from elements in the presence of a medium. Light is an agitator, traveling at the rate of twelve millions of miles per minute: it so agitates the elements that spirits can not gather and use them. There is not a reader of this book who can sleep as well in the light as in the dark. Machinery will run more easily and with less friction in the dark than in the light. If spirits can not sufficiently control elements to appear in a physical form as well in a lighted as in a partially darkened room, how can it be expected that they can pick knots, or chemically separate and join together particles of iron or steel, as well in a lighted room as in the dark? I yet hope to see Spiritualism reduced to a more perfect science when these things can be done in the light.

QUERY NO. 11.

Is Spiritualism sometimes immoral?

Answer. No, never. Always directly to the contrary. Yet mediumship may sometimes call into activity the slumbering devils of the organism. I do not understand that mediumship ever does more than to arouse the latent powers of the organism. Mediumship quickens. A person with a large front brain will therefore be more intellectual under spirit influence than without it. Mediumship stimulates and calls all the latent qualities of the brain into activity. So a large top brain will be more reverential or devotional under influence than without it. A large back brain, with no frontal brain to balance it, will, of course, be stimulated under influence, and the conduct of the medium will be prompted by the back brain. That being the case, he may be more destructive, combative, or amative under influence than without. Does the reader, from this, draw inference that Spiritualism is bad? That is illogical. The shining of the sun, the falling of the rain and dew, certainly quickens and calls into activity the latent germs of life in the earth. Beans, peas, and potatoes, hyacinths, roses, and dahlias, grow under these combined influences; so does pig-weed and deadly-nightshade. Shall we drag the sun from the heavens, or declare against the summer showers, because they develop thorns, thistles, and poison? Nay, while Spiritual influence develops, and calls into activity that which we call evil in the human organism, it also calls out the good. If a person has the good parts of his organism dwarfed by the theologies of the present and the past, he may, for a time, be worse in his overt acts for becoming mediumistic, yet as sure as mediumship strengthens all there is of the medium, so sure it will eventually bring the moral and spiritual up to balance all other parts of the organism.

QUERY NO. 12.

Why do such spirits as Daniel Webster, Henry Clay, and Theodore Parker dwindle into such insignificance when they manifest through inferior organisms?

Answer. Every communication, at all times, partakes of the nature of the organism through which it comes. I have no doubt that Moses, Solomon, Paul, and Peter were inspired. Yet their inspiration did not destroy their distinctive peculiarities. No one can read the Song of Solomon without deciding that he would have all the wives and concubines he could get. The learning and logic of Paul, and the want of erudition and logic in Peter, are traced through all their inspirations. Inspiration, like water, assumes the shape of that through which it passes. A stream of water, coming through a round hole, will come round; through a flat crevice, will come flat. So let Daniel

Webster throw a flood of inspiration down upon a circle, and it will cause each one to act in part his own peculiar nature. One having a massive brain, with the causality and comparison of Mr. Webster, will manifest Webster. Another, with small intellectual and large veneration, will go to praying, while another, with large mirthfulness, would, in a jocose manner, try to get off the thoughts that were thrown into his mind. Probably the same inspiration on different persons would result in all trying to hand out the same thought; but, while one would hand it out in syllogisms, another would use poetry, another prayer; and so on, to the end of the chapter, each one preserving his peculiarities. Again, we doubt whether Theodore Parker or Daniel Webster ever heard of one in ten of the mediums who profess to be under their control. There are hundreds in the spirit world, who, like many here, love to assume some big name, when by that they can get a hearing that, under other circumstances, they could not get. For my part, I do not care what spirit communicates to me. It may be Jesus Christ, General Jackson, or Jack Brown: all I want is *thought* coming from the spirit world. If Webster, or some one in his name, makes a fool of himself, I will listen to him as to any other fool. If a clown hands out a proposition, the carrying out of which will benefit the world, I will take it with the same gratitude as though it was the voice of Him that sitteth upon the throne.

My hope is that Spiritualists will soon get beyond seeking so many personal tests, and strive earnestly to come into more close communion with the world of spirit, the world of *thought,* of *good*, of *God.*

QUERY NO. 13.

Why is so large a percentage of communications from Indian spirits?

Answer. I think I see why more communications of that character than any other should come to us.

1. The Indian is born here, has always lived here, and now belongs here, and nowhere else. It is therefore natural that in the spirit world he should linger about this country, seldom, if ever, leaving it. Not so with the Europeans: they are emigrants here, and even those who are born here are children or grandchildren of those who emigrated to this country. They are more cosmopolitan, and would incline to roam over the world more than those who never knew or desired any other country than this.

2. Indians have been passing to the spirit world from this country for many thousand years, while it has only been a few hundred years since the first white person launched from this country into the spirit world. The Indian element is still, therefore, the positive element in this country. That being the case, there are more of them to control, and they can do it better, more perfectly, than the whites.

3. In this life, Indians are said to be better magnetizers than the whites. They are more the children of nature, are more in harmony with nature, therefore have more power than others who have spent a lifetime in destroying their natural powers, after the order of eating, drinking, sleeping, and living prescribed by a fashion-loving world.

4. In this life, Caucasians are more apt to have a business, and follow it closely, than Indians; there-

fore would not be so apt to leave their business and come to manifest their powers of controlling media, as would those who could do that better, and yet could not do some other more important work as well.

I believe the rule in the spirit world, as in this, should be to put each one to the highest business he or she is capable of performing. Presidents of colleges can teach children their alphabet; but while there are others who could not preside over colleges, who could succeed quite as well in expounding the mysteries of a, b, c, to the child, it would hardly pay to employ the heads of our universities to do that business. The superintendent of the Pacific Railroad could teach boys to play marbles, or girls to dress dolls, but is it expedient for him to leave his business to do so when there are so many who could do that as well as he? General Grant could have gone into the army as a private; but when privates were so plenty, and good generals so scarce, it was hardly prudent for him to do so. So when there is nothing to do in a circle but to give tests of a life beyond, Indians can, to say the least, demonstrate that as well as could Henry Clay or Daniel Webster, if they were present. So let the Indians come: while they give us a lesson of immortality, we may give them a lesson of progress, and thus we may mutually benefit each other. There is such a thing as preaching the gospel to the dead.

5. There is still one more reason why many communications purport to come from Indians. I can not, —individually I *do not choose to disguise* the fact, — a large percentage of what they call Spiritualism is downright humbuggery. I do not mean by that that mediums in the general are guilty of using deception.

In very many instances it is done without the medium knowing it; yet, I am sorry to say, there are those who knowingly and willfully deceive. Such may not have the ability to represent a truly great man, but find it easy enough to jabber broken English in the name of an Indian. Again, there are deceptions which are not willful. In my experience as a medium, I ever found that what purported to be an Indian spirit came first, then came a devotional spirit, then came a philosopher, who gave evidence of erudition entirely beyond my development or study. I now believe all these manifestations came from one and the same spirit. The influence first came to the back brain, which brought physical strength; made me feel well and good-natured; gave me a desire to talk, but no great ideas, so I jabbered: this kept me negative until the top brain was magnetized by some unseen power, then my thoughts ran in a devotional channel; soon the influence passed to the frontal brain, then I began to philosophize. Under that influence I never failed to have an answer to any question of a philosophical character. The retiring influence usually took me back through the same performance of praying and jabbering. May it not be that this is the case in hundreds of instances where the medium never mistrusts but that he has had a different spirit controlling for every different phase of manifestations.

QUERY NO. 14.

Why do we not more frequently get communications from ancient spirits?

Answer. I must confess my doubts as to whether

Solomon, Solon, Socrates, Plato, Pythagoras, Peter, or Paul ever return to communicate. There are epochs in man's existence, and will be throughout eternity. Each is a birth into a higher condition, — a throwing off of a grosser and putting on of a finer body. Those, therefore, who have been long in spirit life may have died to the spheres immediately connected with the earth existence, and hence not be able to come directly *en rapport* with only earthborn mediums. Furthermore, their work is more for those in spirit life than in earth life. To illustrate: Were I to pass to spirit life, I would leave a wife and four daughters, besides a host of other friends to whom I feel a strong attraction. This would fix my work here in earth life for a time. I would be inclined to seek every opportunity to communicate with and bless my friends yet on earth; but every year would bring a new recruit of my friends to spirit life, thus weakening my earth attractions and strengthening those of spirit life. In the course of threescore and ten years all of my earth friends will have gone into "the better country;" then all my attractions will be there, as a consequence of my work there; hence I shall but seldomly return, especially to gratify the caprice of curiosity-hunters. Possibly I may discover a medium through which I can do a great work, and may for many years work through that source. It is more probable, however, that should my name become great, and carry great authority with it, some other spirit would assume it for the sake of benefiting humanity, than that I shall control very many media five hundred years hence. The fact should not be disguised, that there are spirits who, like Paul, "become all things to all men, if by any means they may save some."

Let this account for ancient spirits not returning. When a spirit gives us the name of Adam, Eve, Tubal Cain, or Vulcan, we put them down, not as the original persons who had these names, but as more modern spirits, who were honored with these or some other names.

QUERY NO. 15.

If spirits are subject to such temptations to impose on the credulous as persons are in this life, and as the answer to the above question would indicate, what good can Spiritualism do?

Answer. In important matters there is a way to test spirits. The divine admonition, " try the spirits," in many cases should be put in practice. In many cases it makes no more difference who the spirit than who the medium is. If we go to the spirit for *thought, for ideas,* we care not what spirit imparts them any more than we care what medium it is through whom a test comes. If we are after a test of individuality, and not simply of spirit existence, *try them.* There are rules by which it can be done. Your mother can speak words to you that no other person can. You should always wait for those words before you recognize her.

As to the direct good of Spiritualism, I answer, whether a test was ever given or not, whether a spirit ever told the truth or not, Spiritualism is a demonstration of an existence beyond this. A man, by telling a falsehood, proves his consciousness and ability to choose between a lie and the truth, hence his ability to tell the truth. Thus Spiritualism demonstrates another world, and that that world is filled with the diversity of character that there is in this, thus indicating that the inhabitants of that country emigrated from this.

QUERY NO. 16.

May not a new scientific discovery spoil all there is of Spiritualism?

Answer. No, it can not. A new discovery may, in some measure, modify many theories respecting Spiritualism, but can not overthrow it. A new scientific discovery may modify the modes of teaching mathematics, but no future discovery in any science will change the fact that two multiplied by two will bring four as a result, or that two added to five will make seven. So whatever discoveries may be made, nothing can overcome the one already made, that we are not dependent on our five senses for all our knowledge; that men have seen through solid walls and granite mountains; that they have heard words spoken a thousand miles distant; have been told by an unseen intelligence something they did not know before. Do you call it "mind reading"? Be it so. It was not done with the physical senses; then there are spiritual senses which bid defiance to all the laws governing gross matter. If they do that, and it is proved by the spiritual phenomena, then this spiritual sense bids defiance to death, and *Immortality is triumphant.*

CHAPTER VII.

ACTS OF THE APOSTLES AND SPIRITUALISM.

An interesting book. — Then and now, the Analogy. — A solemn Warning. — Skepticism of the disciples. — "Infallible Proof." — Better Manifestations To-day. — The waiting Time. — The Promise. — What is the Comforter? — Jesus' coming. — The Holy Ghost. — The two Men. — Synopsis of Acts II. — The Cripple healed. — How it was done. — Peter in Court. — Admissions of his Adversaries. — House and Furniture shaken. — Ananias and Sapphira. — Shadow Cures. — The Same now. — Case in St. Louis. — Apostles imprisoned. — Liberated by Spirits. — Report of the Committee. — A modern Case. — A "Mysterious Man." — Stephen's Sermon. — Stephen a Clairvoyant. — Assassination of Stephen. — Peter as a developing Medium. — Simon does not understand the Matter. — Philip a Medium. — Angels talk to him. — A Spirit carries him away. — Author carried by Spirits. — Another Case. — A new Star.

ONE of the most interesting books in the Bible is the one which, in our English translations is called the *Acts of the Apostles.* A more correct rendering would have been the "*Practice of the Apostles.*"

No person, who believes at all in apostolic example, can refrain from admiring that book, as it is the only one that gives us anything of an idea of apostolic practices. It is, however, not for the purpose of exhibiting the minutiæ of apostolic preaching and example that this chapter is written, but to exhibit their sayings and doings on the one question of Spiritualism, and the analogy in their and our relation to the world. Bible believers may draw great profit from such a lesson.

Before commencing a commentary on this Book of

Acts, I would call attention to an apostolic warning. When the Jews disputed the phenomena attending the new religion, Paul used the words of the prophets as follows (Acts xiii. 40, 41): "Beware, therefore, lest that come upon you, which is spoken of in the prophets. Behold, ye despisers, and wonder, and perish; for I work a work in your days, a work which ye shall in no wise believe, though a man declare it unto you."

From this we perceive that it was hard to get a skeptical sectarian to believe in the work [manifestations] of the apostle's day. This skepticism does not seem to have been confined to the outside world; even the disciples were doubtful on many of the manifestations they themselves witnessed. It was said of those who were Jesus' most intimate earthly companions (Matt. xxviii. 16, 17), "Then the eleven disciples went away into Galilee, into a mountain where Jesus had appointed them. And when they saw him, they worshiped him: but some doubted."

While some doubted, others believed the manifestations to be entirely conclusive. The writer of the book under consideration, in speaking of the manifestations to the apostles, says, "Until the day in which he was taken up, after that he, through the Holy Ghost, had given commandments unto the apostles whom he had chosen. To whom also he showed himself alive, after his passion, by many infallible proofs, being seen of them forty days, and speaking of the things pertaining to the kingdom of God." (Acts i. 2, 3.)

Here the proofs that Jesus was alive are declared to be *infallible:* and what are they? Why, nothing more than that "he showed himself alive," and was *seen* forty days, and *spake*. All of these manifestations, and more, are witnessed at Moravia, N. Y., and other places, every day. Did those referred to in these verses prove that Jesus was alive, then we have all the evidence that could be desired to prove that our friends of yesterday, who to-day are in the spirit world, still live. If that text under examination does not prove that Jesus is alive, then there is no text that does, and Christianity can not be proved.

One more point in this text deserves consideration. This Jesus told his disciples that they should *wait* for the fulfillment of a promise which they had heard from him. That waiting consisted in their forming a circle, and sitting in it until the day of Pentecost, which was ten days from this fortieth day, the last on which Jesus was seen, until seen by Paul some years after. This promise, to which he refers, can be none other than that found in John xiv. 16–26.

There are so many good points in the "promise" and Jesus' comments, that I must trouble the reader with a lengthy extract. "And I will pray the Father, and he shall give you another Comforter, that he may abide with you for ever. Even the spirit of truth, whom the world can not receive, because it seeth him not, neither knoweth him: but ye know him; for he dwelleth with you, and shall be in you. I will not leave you comfortless: I will come to you. Yet a little while, and the world seeth me no more; but ye see me: because I live, ye shall live also. At that day ye shall know that I am in my Father, and ye in me, and I in you. He that hath my commandments and keepeth them, he it is that loveth me: and he that loveth me shall be loved of my Father, and I will love him, and will manifest myself to him. Judas saith unto him, — not Iscariot, — Lord, how is it that thou wilt manifest thyself unto us, and not unto the world? Jesus answered, and said unto him, If a man love me, he will keep my words: and my Father will love him, and we will come unto him, and make our abode with him. He that loveth me not keepeth not my sayings: and the word which ye hear is not mine, but the Father's which sent me. These things have I spoken unto you, being yet present with you. But the Comforter, which is the Holy Ghost, whom the Father will send in my name, he shall teach you all things, and bring all things to your remembrance, whatsoever I have said unto you."

Here the promise is of a Comforter: but who is the Comforter? "Even the spirit of truth." That may refer simply to a spirit *power*, and not imply any definite spirit. The next sentence, however, does not. The expression, "Whom the world can not receive, because it seeth *him* not, neither knoweth him," was a proof of clairvoyant power, by which they could see and recognize the spirit, here called the "spirit of truth," and the "comforter." Let it be observed, also, that the spirit here introduced is spoken of as the third person, singular number, and masculine gender. After this, Jesus more than intimates that he himself will be the spirit that they will see and recognize, and the world will not see. "I will come to you," is a positive promise that can not be misunderstood. Even this is not the best part of this promise. He will come as the spirits do at Moravia, so that he can be seen. "The world seeth me no more, but ye see me; because I live, ye shall live also." What could be plainer? Surely nothing, unless it is another sentence in the same promise. "*I will manifest myself to him.*" That was a puzzler to Judas. He could not see how a dead man could manifest himself, so he asks, "How is it that thou wilt manifest thyself unto us, and not to the world?" How many there are to-day who put the same question, reversing the order. Why can't I see spirits as well as others?

This Comforter Jesus defines to be the Holy Ghost: Greek, *Pneumatos Hagion:* that is, good spirit. What so appropriate a comforter as a good spirit? This good spirit, or Holy Ghost, is to *teach*, and bring things to their remembrance. How glorious the harmony between that text and the manifestations of to-day!

But I must return to the Book of Acts, and try to confine this chapter to a consideration of the Spiritualism of that book. Even the first chapter, before the apostles enter upon their ministry at all, has the following record: "And while they looked steadfastly toward heaven, as he went up, behold two men stood by them in white apparel, which also said, Ye men of Galilee, why stand ye gazing up into heaven? This same Jesus, which is taken up from you into heaven, shall so come in like manner as ye have seen him go into heaven." (Acts i. 10, 11.)

These two beings, who stood by the eleven, as their visions were opened to see Jesus ascend, were called *men*. They were men, but not men in the flesh. Their description and garments correspond exactly with a majority of the descriptions of spirits to-day. But these men spake: "This same Jesus," &c. This Spiritualists would call a spirit voice.

ACTS OF THE APOSTLES AND SPIRITUALISM. 179

In a former volume I have thoroughly overhauled the second chapter of Acts, so here I shall do no more than make the briefest statement of the evidence it contains.

1. The Holy Ghost, or good spirit, came and lit upon the mediums.

2. A *diversity* of tongues appeared to *each* of the mediums, enabling each to address strangers in their own language.

3. Peter, after meeting the objection urged by the opponents, that these mediums were drunk, quotes the prophecy of Joel to prove that manifestations of a spiritual character were to occur in this dispensation.

4. He tells them that Jesus, whom he calls "a man approved of God" (not a God), "shed forth what you see and hear."

5. He exhorts the people to repent, and put themselves in a condition to receive the gift of the Holy Ghost, informing them that the promise of the Holy Ghost extended to them and their children, and *all* who are called.

6. "And fear came upon every soul, and many wonders and signs were done by the apostles." (v. 43.) These wonders and signs were just what Jesus had promised should attend the believer, and such, probably, as attend modern mediums.

The next manifestation indicated in the practice of the apostles is recorded in Acts iii. 1–8. "Now Peter and John went up together into the temple, at the hour of prayer, being the ninth hour. And a certain man, lame from his mother's womb, was carried, whom they laid daily at the gate of the temple which is called Beautiful, to ask alms of them that entered into the temple, who, seeing Peter and John about to go into the temple, asked an alms. And Peter, fastening his eyes upon him with John, said, Look on us. And he gave heed unto them, expecting to receive something of them. Then Peter said, Silver and gold have I none; but such as I have give I thee: In the name of Jesus Christ of Nazareth, rise up and walk. And he took him by the right hand, and lifted him up: and immediately his feet and ankle bones received strength. And he, leaping up, stood, and walked, and entered with them into the temple, walking, and leaping, and praising God."

The facts of healing by spirit power are now so numerous that I need not quote circumstances parallel to this. A word might be said on the mode of performing this cure.

1. Peter fastened his eyes on the cripple.
2. He commanded the cripple to look on him.
3. He used the name of Jesus, the one whom he supposed to be his controlling influence, as a charm. They, by looking at each other, as recorded in this instance, were brought into psychologic communication. The use of the name of "the man approved of God by signs and wonders," rendered the patient negative, and consequently receptive — more so, probably, because of his frequent recent appearances. When the people rushed together, astonished at the wonderful phenomenon, Peter explained that he was not the power by which the cripple was healed. He was only an instrument in the hands of spirit powers. His words are (v. 12), "Ye men of Israel, why marvel ye at this? or why look ye so earnestly on us, as

though by our own power or holiness we had made this man to walk?"

In the next chapter, Peter is brought before a tribunal to explain the phenomenon. His answer is (v. 9, 10), "If we this day be examined of the good deed done to the impotent man, by what means he is made whole; be it known unto you all, and to all the people of Israel, that by the name of Jesus Christ of Nazareth, whom ye crucified, whom God raised from the dead, even by him doth this man stand here before you whole."

The full admission of the people, that there was a supermundane power with these mediums, also an ability to preach, though they were unlearned and ignorant men, is recorded in the following (v. 16): "What shall we do to these men? for that indeed a notable miracle hath been done by them, is manifest to all them that dwell in Jerusalem; and we can not deny it. But that it spread no further among the people, let us straightly threaten them, that they speak henceforth to no man in this name."

The next wonder wrought by the mediumship of these men, is of the same kind as that of moving chairs, tables, and pianos. It is recorded in verse 31 of the same chapter. "And when they had prayed, the place was shaken where they were assembled together; and they were all filled with the Holy Ghost, and they spake the word of God with boldness."

This phenomena occurred at what the churches would call a prayer meeting. Spiritualists would call it a circle. No comment is needed. It was a spirit manifestation — nothing more.

In Acts v. 1–10 is the circumstance of Ananias and Sapphira trying to deceive the influences operating through the mediumship of Peter. Peter, being a clairvoyant, could not be deceived. A physiologic power, undoubtedly from the angel world, killed them both. Thus they are made a warning to all others to deal honestly, especially in dealing with risen friends. The extract, like many others in the Book of Acts, is too lengthy for a place in this volume.

In verse 12–16 of this chapter is another instance of the great healing power manifest through the mediumship of those apostles. The following is the record: "And by the hands of the apostles were many signs and wonders wrought among the people; (and they were all with one accord in Solomon's porch: and of the rest durst no man join himself to them: but the people magnified them: and believers were the more added to the Lord, multitudes both of men and women;) insomuch that they brought forth the sick into the streets, and laid them on beds and couches, that at the least the shadow of Peter passing by night overshadow some of them."

I do not think the recorder of the Acts of the Apostles would pretend that there was any virtue in Peter's shadow passing over the sick people. The virtue was in their getting near enough to him to come in communication with his healing power. If this healing was done by a miraculous power from God, instead of a healing power from the spirit world, which they are able to use in the immediate atmosphere of the medium, why have them pass within the shadow of Peter? Why must they touch the hem of Jesus' garment?

This power I have seen in modern Spiritualism several times. In St. Louis, Mo., when preaching and healing, a lady who had been a long time sick was brought into the meeting, for the purpose of having me try my healing power on her. After meeting, when she was introduced, she said, " You have been recommended to me as a healing medium, and I came here to be treated of a disease of long standing. I have been a great sufferer for several years, and seldom go out of the house. I suffered intensely when I came in here this morning. But there was something in your magnetism, or your discourse, which has entirely relieved, and I trust cured me." The lady attended my meetings for five Sundays, and took no other medicine. The magnetism imparted in the delivery of my discourses effected the cure. In the above record we are informed that "unclean spirits were cast out." Were the same thing recorded in modern Spiritualism, it would be, "Undeveloped spirits were cast out." Such manifestations were not to be tolerated, so the writer adds: "Then the high priest rose up, and all they that were with him (which is the sect of the Sadducees), and were filled with indignation. And laid their hands on the apostles, and put them in the common prison." (vs. 17, 18.)

When spirits that understand their business have such mediums as these early Christians, how useless are bars, gates, and handcuffs. Luke goes on to say, "But the angel of the Lord by night opened the prison doors, and brought them forth, and said, Go, stand and speak in the temple to the people all the words of this life." (vs. 19, 20.)

The keepers had watched this prison all night, but somehow the spirits got their mediums out unobserved. The committee appointed the next day to investigate the affair, said, "The prison truly found we shut with all safety, and the keepers standing without before the doors: but when we had opened, we found no man within." (vs. 22.)

Probably no Christian would dispute this story. Angels had the power to let their mediums out of prison, but when similar stories are now related, it is entirely too great a stretch of credulity to believe it. "Consistency is a jewel." Will those who believe these men were let out of prison, believe the same story about mediums in the United States? We have sworn testimony that Mr. Rand was let out of the Oswego, N. Y., jail by spirits. This gentleman had been incarcerated for giving tangible evidence of Spiritualism.

There is enough in the sixth chapter of Acts to convince the unbeliever that its hero, Stephen, was a medium. Verse 8 shows him to be one of the "mysterious men" of his times. Its words are, "And Stephen, full of faith and power, did great wonders and miracles among the people."

Verse 15 says, "And all that sat in the council, looking steadfastly on him, saw his face, as it had been the face of an angel." Nearly all Spiritualists have seen the countenances of mediums lighted up in the same way, in their inspired moments. In this condition Stephen gave the discourse which follows in the next chapter. In that memorable discourse, Stephen makes the following reference to Moses and his mediumship: "And when forty years were expired, there appeared to him in the wilderness of Mount Sinai, an angel of the Lord, in a flame in a bush."

This first Christian martyr relates this incident of Moses seeing and talking with an angel, surrounded with a spirit light, without any apparent consciousness that he was relating anything wonderful. After pursuing this course of argument as far as profitable, he shows the opposition that always has obtained against present manifestations, and compares them to their fathers, who put the mediums of their times to death. His language is, " Which of the prophets have not your fathers persecuted? and they have slain them which showed before of the coming of the Just One ; of whom ye have been now the betrayers and murderers ; who have received the law by the disposition of angels, and have not kept it." (vs. 51-53.)

" Ye do always resist the Holy Ghost." How true! Every generation has its worshipers of past generations: these usually resist the manifestations of their own day. " Ye received the law by the disposition of angels, and have not kept it." What a flood of light that throws on the Old Testament. Instead of the God of the universe personally coming down, and speaking his law in the hearing of all Israel, and writing it with his own finger, we have Jehovah, an angel, the spirit of a dead man, manifesting this interest in behalf of his earth friends.

This " Holy Ghost," that enabled Stephen to talk at once so eloquently and truthfully, also rendered him clairvoyant, so that he could see the " glory of God." We would call it the splendor of the other world, and his old friend Jesus, standing on the right hand of some one he supposed to be God. The record is as follows: "But he, being full of the Holy Ghost, looked up steadfastly into heaven, and saw the glory of God, and Jesus standing on the right hand of God, and said, Behold, I see the heavens opened, and the Son of man standing on the right hand of God."

This clairvoyant manifestation and eloquent discourse, referring in such glowing terms to his friend Jesus, of whom he says they were betrayers and murderers (vs. 52), was too much for this religious mob. He was assassinated on the spot.

In Acts viii. 6, 7, we read, "And the people, with one accord, gave heed unto those things which Philip spoke, hearing and seeing the miracles which he did. For unclean spirits, crying with loud voices, came out of many that were possessed with them; and many taken with palsies, and that were lame, were healed."

In another place I will show that these unclean spirits that were cast out were none other than the spirits of dead men. The miracles would only be called wonderful manifestations, if they occurred to-day. The healing of palsies and cripples is to-day being repeated in many places in this country.

In verses 17-21 the writer says, "Then laid they their hands on them, and they received the Holy Ghost. And when Simon saw that through laying on of the apostles' hands the Holy Ghost was given, he offered them money, saying, Give me also this power, that on whomsoever I lay hands, he may receive the Holy Ghost. But Peter said unto him, Thy money perish with thee, because thou hast thought that the gift of God may be purchased with money. Thou hast neither part nor lot in this matter: for thy heart is not right in the sight of God."

The first lesson here taught is, that "the Holy Ghost, or medium power," was imparted by having the apostles' hands laid on the ones to be developed. The Hon. John Hay, of Texas, is now a developing medium, who does nothing else but go from place to place and develop mediums, by putting his hands on them. He, being *en rapport* with the spirit world, brings subjects in closer connection with spirits, by himself acting as a conductor to bring Heaven's blessings to them.

The second lesson taught in this chapter was, that Simon, though a medium, did not understand developing mediumship. He was not a developing medium, and supposed the power could be purchased with money. The third lesson is, that money can not purchase this gift. If the person has not the organism for it — is not naturally a medium, though he might offer all the gold in California, he has "neither part nor lot in this matter."

Simon was not alone in not being a developing medium. Philip, the great preacher and healer, brought to view in a former part of this chapter, lacked this power. So when those who were made believers by Philip's preaching and works, were developed as mediums, developing mediums had that work to do. Verses 14 and 15 say, "Now when the apostles which were at Jerusalem heard that Samaria had received the word of God, they sent unto them Peter and John, who, when they were come down, prayed for them, that they might receive the Holy Ghost."

The angels conversed with Philip as freely as they ever do now with any mediums. In verse 26 of this chapter we read, "And the angel of the Lord spake unto Philip, saying, Arise, and go toward the south, unto the way that goeth down from Jerusalem unto Gaza, which is desert."

The man who was riding in the chariot was converted and baptized. Then occurred a wonderful physical manifestation, recorded in the following words: "And when they were come up out of the water, the spirit of the Lord caught away Philip, and the eunuch saw him no more, and he went on his way rejoicing. But Philip was found at Azotas: and passing through, he preached in all the cities until he came to Cæsarea."

I find hundreds of persons to-day, who have no trouble at all in believing this declaration, who would not believe me under oath, when I tell them that I have been carried around a room sixteen feet square, by spirit power alone. When I state, and prove by good witnesses, that Andrew Potts, of Harrisburg, Penn., was carried by the spirits from Mechanicsburg to Harrisburg, a distance, I think, of twenty-two miles, inside of four minutes, I will be called a credulous fool, and my witnesses knavish liars. O, that church people could be induced to believe that the same God who superintended matters in the days of Philip, still lives. How soon would they learn that, "The thing that hath been, it is that which shall be: and that which is done is that which shall be done; and there is no new thing under the sun. Is there any thing whereof it may be said, See, this is new ? It hath been already, of old time, which was before us." (Eccl. i. 9, 10.)

This Book of Acts now introduces another character, who becomes so much of a *star* that all others are eclipsed. The reader needs rest and a chance for reflection before he is introduced, so permit me to continue the argument in a new chapter.

CHAPTER VIII.

MORE OF THE SAME.

Saul of Tarsus. — A good Manifestation. — The Points stated. — Ananias a Medium. — Did Paul see Jesus? — Another Case of healing. — Reanimation of Dorcas. — Cornelius's Vision. — A Test. — Peter's Entrancement. — Another Test. — Angel, Spirit, Man. — Peter's preaching. — Spirits eating and drinking. — A second Edition of Pentecost. — Peter's Defence before his Jewish Brethren. — Agabus prophesies under Spirit Power. — Peter released by Spirits. — Particulars of the Case. — Peter at the Gate, his Angel. — Is this true? — Elymas's psychological Blindness. — Paul on the Appearance of Jesus. — Paul heals a Cripple. — Narrative of Paul and Barnabas. — Who is the Man of Macedonia? — Who is the Lord? — Paul and the female Medium. — Who was the Spirit cast out? — Paul and Silas let out of Jail. — Prison shaken and Bands fall off in the Dark. — Iron Rings removed. — Strange Gods. — Apotheosized Men. — Heathen Gods once Men. — Developing Circle at Ephesus. — " Handkerchiefs and Aprons." — A Minister denying his Bible. — The Spirits and the Sons of Sceval. — An Accident. — Paul prophesies. — Another Medium prophesies. — Paul relates his spiritual Experience. — Paul in a Trance. — Takes sides with the Pharisees. — Communication to the Sailors. — A Ship saved by Spirits. — Among Barbarians. — A Snake Bite. — Success as a Healer. — A few Questions. — A word of Warning.

NEARLY all of the remainder of the Book of Acts is devoted to the history of one of the most wonderful mediums of ancient times. He was formerly called Saul of Tarsus, but for reasons not necessary to name here, his name was afterward changed to Paul.

In chapter ix. 3–9, is the account of the wonderful manifestation which took this young and able lawyer out of the ranks of the opposition, and made a believer and medium of him. It reads as follows: " And as he journeyed, he came near Damascus: and suddenly there shined round about him a light from heaven: And he fell to the earth, and heard a voice saying unto him, Saul, Saul, why persecutest thou me? And he said, Who art thou, Lord? And the Lord said, I am Jesus, whom thou persecutest: it is hard for thee to kick against the pricks. And he, trembling and astonished, said, Lord, what wilt thou have me to do? And the Lord said unto him, Arise, and go into the city, and it shall be told thee what thou must do. And the men which journeyed with him stood speechless, hearing a voice, but seeing no man. And Saul arose from the earth; and when his eyes were opened, he saw no man: but they led him by the hand, and brought him into Damascus. And he was three days without sight, and neither did eat nor drink."

Spiritualists claim that every point in this narrative meets its resemblance in modern Spiritualism. The following points are worth noting.

1. "A light from heaven," that is, a spirit light, appeared.

2. "The voice of Jesus," that is, a spirit voice, called out, "Saul, Saul, why persecutest thou me?"

3. Paul saw the spirit of Jesus, but the others did not.

4. "And when his eyes were opened." This implies that his eyes were closed when he saw Jesus, so that he did not see with his natural eyes, but as mediums generally see spirits, with his spiritual vision.

This man, while physically blind, "saw in a vision a man named Ananias coming and putting his hands on him that he might receive his sight." (vs. 12.)

This spiritual vision was fulfilled in the following manner: —

"And Ananias went his way, and entered into the house; and putting his hands on him, said, Brother Saul, the Lord, even Jesus, that appeared unto thee in the way as thou camest, hath sent me, that thou mightest receive thy sight, and be filled with the Holy Ghost. And immediately there fell from his eyes as it had been scales: and he received his sight forthwith, and arose, and was baptized." (vs. 17, 18.)

In these verses, beside the fulfillment of this mission, we have the positive testimony that Jesus appeared to Paul. I would like to ask all who look for the second appearing of Jesus, which appearing this was? The fact is, there is no evidence that Jesus ever did, or ever will, appear in any other way than that in which our dead friends appear to-day. Another evidence that Paul really saw Jesus is found in verse 27: "But Barnabas took him, and brought him to the apostles, and declared unto them how that he had seen the Lord in the way, and that he had spoken to him, and how he had preached boldly at Damascus in the name of Jesus.

This was evidently the case, afterward referred to by Paul, when he said, "And last of all he was seen of me also, as of one born out of due time." (1 Cor. xv. 8.)

In verses 33 and 34 of Acts ix., is the record of another wonderful case of healing by Peter.

"And there he found a certain man named Æneas, which had kept his bed eight years, and was sick of the palsy; and Peter said unto Æneas, Jesus Christ maketh thee whole; arise, and make thy bed. And he arose immediately."

The next instance of healing recorded in the Book is that of Dorcas, who was supposed to have been dead. Peter's mediumship was sufficient to overcome even supposed death. The author of this book of *actions*, records the matter as follows: —

"But Peter put them all forth, and kneeled down, and prayed: and turning him to the body, said, Tabitha, arise. And she opened her eyes, and when she saw Peter she sat up. And he gave her his hand, and lifted her up, and when he had called the saints and the widows, he presented her alive."

The tenth chapter of the Book under review opens with the history of Cornelius, a devout Gentile. It relates a manifestation which, taken in all of its parts, is so wonderful and so similar to modern manifestations, that I must give it more than a passing notice. It says of Cornelius, "He saw in a vision, evidently about the ninth hour of the day, an angel of God coming in to him, and saying unto him, Cornelius. And when he looked on him, he was afraid, and said, What is it, Lord? And he said unto him, Thy prayers and thine alms are come up for a memorial before God. And now send men to Joppa, and call for one Simon, whose surname is Peter." (vs. 3, 5.)

This part of the manifestation does not contain much proof of Spiritualism, aside from the fact that Cornelius saw and talked with an angel who told him of Peter, and where he lived. The sequel proved this communication to be correct. When the other parts of this narrative are brought to bear, the strength of the evidence in it will appear. Cornelius, determined to know of the truth of his vision, immediately dispatched men to see whether the angels had told the truth. But, before the men arrived, Peter, by spirit power, learned the particulars.

"On the morrow, as they went on their journey, and drew nigh unto the city, Peter went up upon the house-top to pray about the sixth hour: and he became very hungry, and would have eaten: but while they made ready, he fell into a trance, and saw heaven opened, and a certain vessel descending unto him, as it had been a great sheet knit at the four corners, and let down to the earth: wherein were all manner of fourfooted beasts of the earth, and wild beasts, and creeping things, and fowls of the air. And there came a voice to him, Rise, Peter; kill, and eat. But Peter said, Not so, Lord; for I have never eaten anything that is common or unclean. And the voice spake unto him again the second time, What God hath cleansed, that call not thou common. This was done thrice: and the vessel was received up again into heaven. Now while Peter doubted in himself what this vision which he had seen should mean, behold, the men which were sent from Cornelius had made inquiry for Simon's house, and stood before the gate, and called, and asked whether Simon, which was surnamed Peter, were lodged there. While Peter thought on the vision, the Spirit said unto him, Behold, three men seek thee. Arise, therefore, and get thee down, and go with them, doubting nothing: for I have sent them. Then Peter went down to the men which were sent unto him from Cornelius; and said, Behold, I am he whom ye seek: what is the cause wherefore ye are come?" (vs. 9-21.)

MORE OF THE SAME. 195

The case now begins to look stronger, but its strength has not yet appeared. From verse 10 we learn that Peter fell into a trance: no one at all acquainted with Spiritualism will have any trouble in understanding that. In verses 13 and 15 spirit voices spoke to him. In verse 19 the declaration is positive that this " voice which had been talking was a *spirit voice*, as it was a spirit that was doing the talking. In verse 20 the spirit says, "I have sent them (the men who were seeking Peter). But these men were sent by an angel. (See vs. 3.) Therefore, the angel of verse 3 was the spirit of verse 20. In verse 21 Peter gives these men a test by announcing himself as being the man whom they were seeking.

This matter still grows stronger as we proceed. Peter went with these men, as the spirit had bidden him. When he got to the house of Cornelius, and asked to what intent he had been sent for, Cornelius answered, "Four days ago I was fasting until this hour; and at the ninth hour I prayed in my house, and, behold, a man stood before me in bright clothing, and said, Cornelius, thy prayer is heard, and thine alms are had in remembrance in the sight of God. Send, therefore, to Joppa, and call hither Simon, whose surname is Peter; he is lodged in the house of one Simon a tanner by the seaside: who, when he cometh, shall speak unto thee." (vs. 30–32.)

Here, it will be observed, that Cornelius said, "*Behold, a man in bright clothing stood before me.*" In verse 20 that "man" announced himself to Peter as a spirit man. This man in bright clothing was " the angel of God." Thus we find another proof that the angels of the Bible, like the demons and gods of the heathens, were the spirits of men, or spirit men.

Peter commences his preaching immediately, during which he relates the circumstance of the death, and the wonderful phenomena of the appearances of Jesus after his death. He says, "Him God raised up the third day, and showed him openly; not to all the people, but unto witnesses chosen before of God, even to us, who did eat and drink with him after he rose from the dead." (vs. 40, 41.)

God showed Jesus openly: but how, and to whom? I answer, his appearance was always under the same conditions that spirits are seen now. "Not to all the people," is Peter's language. Who were those "witnesses chosen"? If they lived to-day they would be called clairvoyants. But Jesus ate and drank after he arose from the dead. Probably he did. Spirits do that almost every day in the circles of Mrs. Keigwin, of Jeffersonville, Ind. The phenomena which attended or followed Peter's preaching were similar to those of the day of Pentecost. The record says, "While Peter yet spake these words, the Holy Ghost fell on all them which heard the word. And they of the circumcision which believed were astonished, as many as came with Peter, because that on the Gentiles also was poured out the gift of the Holy Ghost. For they heard them speak with tongues, and magnify God." (vs. 44-46.) As this manifestation is so similar to that of Pentecost, comment is needless.

This matter does not terminate thus. Peter's Jewish brethren were not satisfied. They supposed these phenomena belonged exclusively to the circumcision, and hence called Peter to account for preaching the gospel to the Gentiles. I make two extracts from Peter's defence. In chapter xi. 5, he says, "I was in the city of Joppa, praying: and in a trance I saw a vision: a certain vessel descend, as it had been a great sheet, let down from heaven by four corners; and it came even to me." Here is the relation of both a "trance and a vision." In verses 12, 13 he says, "And the spirit bade me go with them, nothing doubting. Moreover these six brethren accompanied me, and we entered into the man's house: and he showed us how he had seen an angel in his house, which stood and said unto him, Send men to Joppa, and call for Simon, whose surname is Peter." I do not like to dispute the words of Peter; but if the reader will take the pains to turn back to Acts x. 30, he will read Cornelius' story. There is not one word in it about an angel. He says, "Behold, a man stood before me in bright clothing," &c. Thus we have it again, that which Cornelius calls a man, Peter calls an angel, and in verse 19, a spirit. The fact is, men, when they pass into the other world, become angels or spirits.

I cannot pass from this chapter without quoting verses 27, 28: "And in these days came prophets from Jerusalem unto Antioch. And there stood up one of them named Agabus, and signified by the spirit that there should be great dearth throughout all the world: which came to pass in the days of Claudius Cæsar."

Why are none of these examples followed in the church to-day? Where are the church's prophets? How thoroughly do churches, in their practice, deny the power of godliness. It was a spirit that enabled this Agabus to prophecy.

In Acts xii. is one of the most wonderful cases of spirit manifestation recorded in ancient or modern history. Though the extract is lengthy, I see no place to divide it, and therefore I give it entire.

"Peter, therefore, was kept in prison: but prayer was made without ceasing of the church unto God for him. And when Herod would have brought him forth, the same night Peter was sleeping between two soldiers, bound with two chains: and the keepers before the door kept the prison. And, behold, the angel of the Lord came upon him, and a light shined in the prison: and he smote Peter on the side, and raised him up, saying, Arise up quickly. And his chains fell off from his hands. And the angel said unto him, Gird thyself, and bind on thy sandals. And so he did. And he saith unto him, Cast thy garment about thee, and follow me. And he went out, and followed him; and wist not that it was true which was done by the angel; but thought he saw a vision. When they were past the first and the second ward, they came unto the iron gate that leadeth unto the city; which opened to them of his own accord: and they went out, and passed on through one street; and forthwith the angel departed from him. And when Peter was come to himself, he said, Now I know of a surety, that the Lord hath sent his angel, and hath delivered me out of the hand of Herod, and from all the expectation of the people of the Jews. And when he had considered the thing, he came to the house of Mary the mother of John, whose surname was Mark; where many were gathered together praying. And as Peter knocked at the door of the gate, a damsel came to hearken, named Rhoda. And when she knew Peter's voice, she opened not the gate for gladness, but ran in, and told how Peter stood before the gate. And they said unto her, Thou art mad. But she constantly affirmed that it was even so. Then said they, It is his angel. But Peter continued knocking: and when they had opened the door, and saw him, they were astonished."

Notice the points of similarity in this and modern Spiritualism.

1. After stating that Peter was put into prison, and bound with chains, and put between soldiers to sleep, and keepers placed at the door, an angel or spirit went into the prison.

2. "A light shined in the prison." This was what we call a "spirit light."

3. When the angel smote Peter on the side and raised him up, the chains fell off. Such manifestations occur with the Davenports and others.

4. "The iron gate opened of its own accord." I think this is a mistake. Gates do not have accord. Where there is no mind there can be no accord. Peter was simply not sufficiently clairvoyant to see the angel who opened the gate. Modern spirit mediums, who have been let out of prison, have not been able to see the angel who opened the door.

5. Some power led Peter to where his brethren were holding a prayer-meeting or circle.

6. When he got to the house, and knocked at the door, and the little girl recognized him, those who did not believe the child first urged that she was insane. They could not see how it was possible that iron chains could be taken off of Peter, and an iron door opened.

After arguing a few moments, they decided that the girl was not mad, but that what she saw and they heard rapping at the gate was "his angel." Several times in the course of this and a former volume I have shown that angels were the spirits of dead men. Jesus once said, "Take heed that ye despise not one of these little ones; for I say unto you, That in heaven their angels do always behold the face of my Father which is in heaven." (Matt. xviii. 10.)

The early church believed, as many do now, that each person was under the training of an angel. They believed also that persons grew to look like the angels under whose charge they were. This may account for their supposing that it was Peter's angel rather than Peter himself that stood rapping at the gate. If they had not believed that spirits could rap, why should they say, "It is his angel"?

This truly wonderful manifestation is in every part corroborated by modern Spiritualism. The Davenports, Dewitt C. Hough, Laura V. Ellis, and others, have similar manifestations. Why shall I believe what my eyes have seen, and refuse to believe that others have experienced the same, or witnessed similar phenomena? Or why shall I believe this Biblical story, and refuse to believe the occurrences of to-day which so fully corroborate it?

In Acts xiii. 8–11, we have the following: "Then Saul (who also is called Paul), filled with the Holy Ghost, set his eyes on him, and said, O full of all subtilty and all mischief, thou child of the devil, thou enemy of all righteousness, wilt thou not cease to pervert the right ways of the Lord? And now, behold, the hand of the Lord is upon thee, and thou shalt be blind, not seeing the sun for a season. And immediately there fell on him a mist and a darkness, and he went about seeking some to lead him by the hand."

It does seem that mediums in those days were, as some are now, jealous of each other. Elymas undertook to work against Paul. Paul was the best medium, and being filled with the Holy Ghost (another expression for spirit influence), "he set his eyes on him," and while looking him in the eye, pronounced a curse on him, rendering him blind for a season. This I have seen done psychologically many times. The blindness, however, does not continue, as it did not in this case. Being only psychological, it lasts only while the psychologic spell lasts.

In this chapter, Paul delivers a discourse, from which I make a short extract: " And when they had fulfilled all that was written of him, they took him down from the tree, and laid him in a sepulchre. But God raised him from the dead : and he was seen many days of them which came up with him from Galilee to Jerusalem, who are his witnesses unto the people."

Jesus is the subject of whom Paul is speaking; "God raised him from the dead." The body was dead, and God raised Jesus from it, or out of it. How does Paul know? He answers, he was *seen*, but not by all the people, as he evidently would have been had his body been raised, but by "certain ones who were his witnesses unto the people." When the people wished to know anything about the appearance of Jesus, they had no way to find out but by consulting those who, from time to time, were enabled to see him after his resurrection. I often wonder how it is that people could ever twist those texts so as to make them teach a reorganization and re-living of the body rather than the spiritual phenomena.

In Acts xiv. is a case of Spiritualism worth recording; it reads as follows: "And there sat a certain man at Lystra, impotent in his feet, being a cripple from his mother's womb, who never had walked: the same heard Paul speak: who steadfastly beholding him, and perceiving that he had faith to be healed, said with a loud voice, Stand upright on thy feet. And he leaped and walked." (vs. 8, 9, 10.)

There are mediums now who could perform as great wonders.

Acts xv. is about the only chapter that does not contain the record of some greater phenomenon than is practised by any of the churches, or any others, save spirit mediums. That gives the narrative of Paul and Barnabas concerning matters not elsewhere recorded. Verse 12 says, "Then all the multitude kept silence, and gave audience to Barnabas and Paul, declaring what miracles and wonders God had wrought among the Gentiles by them."

In those days the whole proof of the ministry seemed to lie in the ability to do works called miracles.

In verse 28, the spirit influence, or good spirit, is referred to as follows: "For it seemed good to the Holy Ghost, and to us, to lay upon you no greater burden than these necessary things."

A manifestation, the origin of which can not easily be mistaken, is recorded in Acts xvi. 6–10. "Now when they had gone throughout Phrygia and the region of Galatia, and were forbidden of the Holy Ghost to preach the word in Asia, after they were come to Mysia, they assayed to go into Bithynia: but the spirit suffered them not. And they, passing by Mysia, came down to Troas. And a vision appeared to Paul in the night: There stood a man of Macedonia, and prayed him, saying, Come over into Macedonia, and help us."

This Holy Ghost that forbade their preaching the word in Asia, was the same spirit that would not allow them to preach in Bithynia. It is probable, too, that this was the man of Macedonia, who said, "Come over and help us." This was a spirit man. Paul was in a spiritual condition when he saw this man, who, by the way, was a Macedonian. This being true, it follows that the spirits of Macedonians can come back and say, "Come over and help us."

What plainer evidence could be required that the "Holy Ghost," "spirit," and "men," are all the same? So, also, are the angels, as proved by the tenth chapter of this book, and the saints, as proved by other portions of the Bible. And from this they gathered that the Lord had called them to Macedonia to preach. Surely the Lord who called them this time was the man of Macedonia.

Reader, permit me to whisper in your ear, that the Lords that figured so extensively throughout the Old and New Testaments, were always either men in the form, or spirits of dead men. In this instance it was the latter. In verses 16–18 of this chapter, is the following record: "And this did she many days. But Paul, being grieved, turned and said to the spirit, I command thee, in the name of Jesus Christ, to come out of her. And he came out the same hour."

Here is another instance of jealousy, and the triumph of the greater over the weaker mediumship. This woman, certainly under this influence, preached the same gospel as that preached by Paul, and recommended Paul and Silas to her friends; but Paul was a crusty old bachelor, who did not believe in having his preaching eclipsed by that of a woman. He had said, "Let your women keep silence in the churches: for it is not permitted unto them to speak; but they are commanded to be under obedience, as also saith the law. And if they will learn anything, let them ask their husbands at home: for it is a shame for women to speak in the church." (1 Cor. xiv. 34, 35.)

Again: "Let your women learn in silence, with all subjection." (1 Tim. ii. 2.)

Paul cast the spirit of divination out of this girl. I do not know why the translators put the word "divination" there. They have put the word Python in the margin, — the Greek word is *Pythones*. Then it was the spirit of Pythones that was driven from this medium. And who was Pythones? I will tell you. Python was a great snake, killed by the god Apollo. But it is not reasonable to suppose that the spirit of a snake obsessed this lady, so we must look further into heathenism for a solution of this question. After Apollo killed Python, he gave the name to an old woman dressed in girls' clothes, who had the power of telling fortunes. So any one who could tell fortunes by power from the dead was afterward called a Pythoness. This spirit of Python either means the spirit of this old lady of heathen fable, or simply spirit power. (See Tooke's "Pantheon," pages 39-44.)

So this case only proves to be one medium casting the spirit of a dead woman out of another. There is jealousy even among the spirits. "The Lord thy God is a jealous God, and his glory he will not give to another."

The next manifestation recorded in this Book is found in verses 26, 27 of this chapter. "And at midnight Paul and Silas prayed, and sang praises unto God: and the prisoners heard them. And suddenly there was a great earthquake, so that the foundations of the prison were shaken: and immediately all the doors were opened, and every one's bands were loosed."

1. This manifestation occurred at midnight, the best time during the twenty-four hours for physical manifestations.

2. "The foundations of the prison were shaken." Is not this a manifestation of a similar kind to that of shaking and tipping of tables, chairs, and pianos?

3. "The doors were opened, and every one's bands were loosed." Whatever power may have opened the doors, the bands were loosed by the same power now used to accomplish the same work. Probably the bands were what now would be called handcuffs. I have been in seances where solid iron rings, so small that the hand could not be forced through them, have been put on and taken off of the medium's arm by spirit power alone. True, in the case of Dewitt C. Hough, and others, these things were done in the dark. So did this occur in the dark. Verse 29 says, "Then he (the jailer) called for a light, and sprang in, and came trembling, and fell down before Paul and Silas."

If I am asked for an explanation of why darkness was required for this manifestation, I can at present only refer to the chapter in this volume entitled "Minor Questions."

In Acts xvii. 18-20, the writer refers to heathen

philosophers, as follows: "Then certain philosophers of the Epicureans, and of the Stoics, encountered him. And some said, What will this babbler say? other some, He seemeth to be a setter forth of strange gods: because he preached unto them Jesus, and the resurrection."

It is not to be inferred from this that Paul preached Jesus as a god; but he preached Jesus and the resurrection. This doctrine was well known among the Grecians. They nearly all believed in what they called the *Apotheosis*, that is, that some men at death were elevated to the position of gods. When Paul preaches the *Anastasis*, that is, the rising of Jesus, they understood him to teach their own doctrine of *apotheosized* men; that Jesus at or about the time of his death had been exalted to be a god. Hence they said Paul's doctrine was that of other and strange gods. As they wanted to get acquainted with this Jesus, whom they regarded as a new god, they invited Paul into their own *Areopagus* to present the evidence of Jesus' *apotheosis*.

Almost every work of Grecian mythology will show their gods to have once been men on earth. Tooke says, "After Ninus had conquered many nations far and near, and built a city, called after his name Nineveh, in a public assembly of the Babylonians he extolled his father Belus, the founder of the empire and city of Babylon, beyond all measure, representing him not only worthy of perpetual honor among all posterity, but also of an immortality among the gods above. He then exhibited a statue of him, curiously and neatly made, to which he commanded them to pay the same reverence that they would have given to Belus while alive. He also appointed it to be a common sanctuary to the miserable, and ordained 'that if at any time an offender should fly to this statue it should not be lawful to force him away to punishment.' This privilege easily procured so great a veneration to the dead prince, that he was thought more than a man, and, therefore, was created a god, and called Jupiter, or, as others write, Saturn of Babylon, where a most magnificent temple was erected to him by his son."—*Pantheon*, p. 18.

On pages 21, 22, the same author says, "And lastly, to this class also we must refer those gods and goddesses by whose help and means, as Cicero says, men advanced to heaven, and obtained a place among the gods; of which sort are the principal virtues, as we shall show in the proper place."

Dr. Campbell says, "From the days of Titan and Saturn, the poetic progeny of Cœlus and Terra, down to Æsculapius, Protius, and Minos, all their gods were the departed spirits of human beings, and were so regarded by the most erudite of the pagans themselves."

Tooke thus describes the earth life of Apollo, page 41: "Apollo was advanced to the highest degree of honor and worship by these four means, viz., by the invention of physic, music, poetry, and rhetoric, which is ascribed to him; and, therefore, he is supposed to preside over the Muses. It is said that he taught the arts of foretelling events, and shooting with arrows; when, therefore, he had benefited mankind infinitely by these favors, they worshiped him as a god."

The next instance to which I shall refer is found in chapter xix. Paul went to Ephesus, and finding some brethren there, "He said unto them, Have ye received the Holy Ghost since ye believed? And they said unto him, We have not so much as heard whether there be any Holy Ghost." (vs. 2.)

That is, he asked them concerning this spiritual influence. They responded they had heard nothing of these manifestations. The truth is, they had been baptized by Apollos, one of John's disciples, who knew nothing of this new development. Paul explained the matter to them, and they formed a developing circle, which resulted in making mediums of them. Dr. Luke, the historian, records the matter as follows: "And when Paul had laid his hands upon them, the Holy Ghost came on them; and they spake with tongues, and prophesied."

Paul next went to Asia to preach, and give manifestations to the Jews and Greeks. Though Luke, the writer of this Book, was a "beloved physician," his jealousy did not prevent his making the following record: " And God wrought special miracles by the hands of Paul: so that from his body were brought unto the sick handkerchiefs or aprons, and the diseases departed from them, and the evil spirits went out of them." (vs. 11, 12.)

Dr. Wilbur, a medium in Chicago, performs many cures by sending magnetized paper to the patient. I myself have removed disease in the same way. The principle is the same as that by which Paul healed in the above instance. In one of my lectures, I once related the circumstance of Dr. Wilbur, curing an obstinate case of dropsy,—a case that doctors had pronounced incurable. The doctor used magnetized paper, *and no other remedy*. A Methodist minister, of small brain and large assurance, was present, who said, "I take it upon myself to pronounce that story a *hoax:* no case of the kind ever occurred." I replied, "I have no witnesses in this audience to prove my story. I will, however, give the names and post-office address of witnesses to which you can refer. I will further state that I know mediums who have healed persons by sending pocket-handkerchiefs to them, and I have printed documents here to show that another medium, whom I never saw, has done the same thing."

To this the minister replied, in substance, as follows: —

"I have no doubt Mr. Hull could furnish witnesses. As he and his friends do not believe in Christianity, they might be induced to testify to almost anything that would forward their cause. So far as printed statements are concerned, he who would tell a lie could be induced to print one. So I would not believe any printed document of the kind. Such things are all printed in the interest of Spiritualism, and must be considered *ex parte* evidence. The humble Christian must trust in Jesus and reject them."

"And yet," I replied, "I must read my printed evidence. If my friend does not believe it, some others may. It is found in the Actions of the Apostles, chapter xiv., verses 11, 12." I then read the verses above quoted, and said, "We allow Methodist ministers to dispute the Bible: such plain historical statements, corroborated as this one is by modern history and my own experience, I cannot dispute."

A case occurs in Acts xix. 13–16, which can not really be classed with apostolic acts, yet as it is a case of spirit obsession, a mediumship that seven exorcists were not able to overcome, I quote it:—

"Then certain of the vagabond Jews, exorcists, took upon them to call over them which had evil spirits the name of the Lord Jesus, saying, We adjure you by Jesus whom Paul preacheth. And there were seven sons of one Sceva, a Jew, and chief of the priests, which did so. And the evil spirit answered and said, Jesus I know, and Paul I know; but who are ye? And the man in whom the evil spirit was leaped on them, and overcame them, and prevailed against them, so that they fled out of that house naked and wounded."

This case of wonderful physical strength under the influence of this evil or undeveloped spirit, is well attested. The next verse says, "And this was known to all the Jews and Greeks also dwelling at Ephesus; and fear fell on them all, and the name of the Lord Jesus was magnified."

In Acts xx. 9–12 is another manifestation of healing. The following is the narrative:—

"And there sat in a window a certain young man named Eutychus, being fallen into a deep sleep: and as Paul was long preaching, he sunk down with sleep, and fell down from the third loft, and was taken up dead. And Paul went down, and fell on him, and embracing him, said, Trouble not yourselves; for his life is in him. When he therefore was come up again, and had broken bread, and eaten, and talked a long while, even till break of day, so he departed. And they brought the young man alive, and were not a little comforted."

In this chapter, the influence called the Holy Ghost,

talks again to Paul. Paul says, "And now, behold, I go bound in the spirit unto Jerusalem, not knowing the things that shall befall me there: save that the Holy Ghost witnesseth in every city, saying that bonds and afflictions abide me." (vs. 22, 23.)

In chapter xxi. 4, the spirit again speaks: "And finding disciples, we tarried there seven days: who said to Paul through the spirit, that he should not go up to Jerusalem."

In verse 11, a spirit influences a medium by the name of Agabus, and gives a prophecy, which the writer refers to as follows: "And when he was come unto us, he took Paul's girdle, and bound his own hands and feet, and said, Thus saith the Holy Ghost, So shall the Jews at Jerusalem bind the man that owneth this girdle, and shall deliver him into the hands of the Gentiles."

This prophecy proved true in all its parts.

In chapter xxii. Paul relates the wonderful phenomenon that converted him, a history of which was given in chapter ix. I have not the space for Paul's lengthy remarks. A brief extract from Ananias's communication to Paul is as follows: "And he said, The God of our fathers hath chosen thee, that thou shouldest know his will, and see that Just One, and shouldest hear the voice of his mouth. For thou shalt be his witness unto all men of what thou hast seen and heard."

In verses 17–21 Paul relates some things Jesus said to him when he was entranced: "And it came to pass, that, when I was come again to Jerusalem, even while I prayed in the temple, I was in a trance; and saw him saying unto me, Make haste, and get thee quickly out of Jerusalem: for they will not receive thy testimony concerning me. And I said, Lord, they know that I imprisoned and beat in every synagogue them that believed on thee: and when the blood of thy martyr Stephen was shed, I also was standing by, and consenting unto his death, and kept the raiment of them that slew him."

In chapter xxiii. 7–10, Paul declares his belief in spirits, and the Pharisees confess their faith that spirits and angels talk with him. "And when he had so said, there arose a dissension between the Pharisees and the Sadducees: and the multitude was divided. For the Sadducees say that there is no resurrection, neither angel, nor spirit: but the Pharisees confess both. And there arose a great cry: and the scribes that were of the Pharisees' part arose, and strove, saying, We find no evil in this man: but if a spirit or an angel hath spoken to him, let us not fight against God."

In chapter xxvii. Paul relates his "perceptions" when at sea. He says to the officers of the ship, on which he was a prisoner, "Sirs, I perceive that this voyage will be with hurt and much damage, not only of the lading and ship, but also of our lives." (vs. 10.)

Paul's warning was not heeded. The *reckless* captain was disobedient to the warning, and, as a consequence, had his vessel *wrecked*.

After their first disaster, the historian says, "But after long abstinence Paul stood forth in the midst of them, and said, Sirs, ye should have hearkened unto me, and not have loosed from Crete, and to have gained this harm and loss. And now I exhort you to be of good cheer: for there shall be no loss of any man's life among you, but of the ship. For there stood by me this night the angel of God, whose I am, and whom I serve, Saying, Fear not, Paul; thou must be brought before Cæsar: and, lo, God hath given thee all them that sail with thee. Wherefore, sirs, be of good cheer: for I believe God, that it shall be even as it was told me. Howbeit we must be cast upon a certain island."

This prophecy proved true, and but for spirit advice, through the organism of Paul, all would have been lost. After the worst of their trouble was over, Paul again uttered a prediction which proved true. Luke records it as follows: "And while the day was coming on, Paul besought them all to take meat, Saying, this is the fourteenth day that ye have tarried, and continued fasting, having taken nothing. Wherefore I pray you to take some meat: for this is for your health: for there shall not an hair fall from the head of any of you." (vs. 33, 34.)

These opponents of Spiritualism, and Paul the Spiritualist, found themselves cast away among barbarians; but they were like the great majority of heathens, a kind and hospitable people. The record says, "And the barbarous people showed us no little kindness; for they kindled a fire, and received us every one, because of the present rain, and because of the cold." (xxviii. 2.)

Following this is the record of a wonderful manifestation. "And when Paul had gathered a bundle of sticks, and laid them on the fire, there came a viper out of the heat, and fastened on his hand. And when the barbarians saw the venomous beast hang on his hand, they said among themselves, No doubt this man is a murderer, whom, though he hath escaped the sea, yet vengeance suffereth not to live. And he shook off the beast into the fire, and felt no harm. Howbeit they looked when he should have swollen, or fallen down dead suddenly; but after they had looked a great while, and saw no harm come to him, they changed their minds, and said that he was a god." (vs. 3–6.)

Comment is needless. It was just what Jesus said should attend the believers. It is just what churches do not, and *can not* do. Thus they prove their infidelity.

Another case of healing is brought to view in this chapter. "And it came to pass, that the father of Publius lay sick of a fever and of a bloody flux: to whom Paul entered in, and prayed, and laid his hands on him, and healed him. So when this was done, others also, which had diseases in the island, came, and were healed. Who also honored us with many honors: and when we departed, they laded us with such things as were necessary." (vs. 8–10.)

These cases of healing were similar to modern Spiritualism. How kind these heathens were! If our Christian Americans would treat the heathen Chinese as these barbarians treated Paul, our religion would stand higher before the world, and the heathen world could respect us more.

Now, patient reader, I have gone through the Book called the *Acts of the Apostles*. I pause to inquire of you, Who imitates the *practice* of these first Christians? Is there an evangelical Christian on earth who follows their example? Are they, or do they, profess to be under the influence of the *Pneumatos Hagion?* Do they speak with other tongues? Do they lay their hands on the sick, and cause them to recover? Where are the cripples they have healed? When did one of them follow the example of Paul and Peter, and go into a trance? Do they have visions? Can they foretell the future, as did Paul on several occasions, after an angel had stood by him and talked with him? In what sense do modern Christians follow apostolic example? Alas, for them! The kingdom of heaven has been taken from them, and given to a nation bringing forth the fruits thereof! They have the form of godliness, but the power, if they ever had it, has departed from them.

O Orthodoxy, I counsel thee to purchase of the spirit world, by humble contrition and sincere repentance, "gold tried in the fire, that thou mayest be rich, and white raiment, that thou mayest be clothed, and that the shame of thy nakedness do not appear, and anoint thine eyes with eye-salve that thou mayest see." He that hath ears to hear, let him hear what the spirit saith unto the churches.

Spiritualists, let us take warning, lest as bad or a worse thing befall us. I tremble for Spiritualism, lest when it becomes popular it should depart from its allegiance to the spirit world. Let us ever be receptive to the influence from our risen friends.

Had I time, and my readers the patience, to go through the whole Bible, as I have the Book of Acts, I could show it all to be but the prototype of the Phenomenal Spiritualism of the Nineteenth Century.

CHAPTER IX.

WHAT IS EVANGELICALISM?

A general Departure from Evangelicalism. — Bible on Infant Damnation. — The Gods of Orthodoxy. — Eternally begotten Son, meaning of. — Eternal Decrees. — Prayer and the Decrees. — Predestination and Reprobation. — Consequences of the Doctrine. — Presbyterian Justice. — The World made of Nothing in six Days. — The Fall of Man. — The Devil in the Snake. — All for God's Glory. — Adam totally depraved. — The Result. — Very God and very Man. — God his own Son and Father. — A naughty Ghost. — Mary God's Mother. — A Pyramid of Absurdities. — Justice satisfied. — No Power to will. — Who are the Called? — Elect Infants. — Doom of Non-professors. — Saved by Christ's Righteousness alone. — Is a second Payment demanded. — Catechisms on Punishment. — Sinfulness of Goodness. — Perseverance of the Saints. — Spiritualism, twenty of its Points of Superiority. — Conclusion.

THIS volume has already grown to nearly the dimensions I had calculated, and I must think of closing; and as I commenced with a chapter devoted to the question, "What is Spiritualism?" how can I more appropriately close the book than with a few thoughts in review of the other side of the question.

Ministers in their sermons and prayers, and authors in their writings nowadays so universally depart from their own religious systems, that a person could not gather the peculiarities of Evangelicalism from what is heard in modern pulpits, and read in modern books. Even a statement of what Evangelicalism is, is often disputed by those who pretend to follow its teachings. Lest religionists should lay this book down with a sneer, and charge of general misrepresentation, I propose to let Evangelicalism state itself. I shall, in the statement, quote from no other authority than the Orthodox Confession of Faith, and the Larger and Shorter Catechims, published by the Presbyterian Board of Publication, 265 Chestnut Street, Philadelphia. This Confession of Faith and these Catechisms are indorsed in the main by all who call themselves Evangelical Christians. Some of the minor points, such as the doctrine of Election, Reprobation, Infant Damnation, and a few others, may not be indorsed by some of the smaller sects of Christians. While Methodists would repudiate the former of these doctrines, John Wesley did assert in his doctrinal tracts that infants were liable to eternal damnation. I do not see why they should not be. The Bible teaches, as clearly as it teaches anything, that infants are liable to suffer under the wrath of God. When Moses gave his command to slay, he prefaced it with a "Thus saith the Lord," and made it read as follows: "Now, therefore, kill every male among the little ones." (Num. xxxi. 17.) If God would, in a fit of anger, make such universal havoc among the little boys, why should he so change as to save them? If he would kill little baby boys, why not send them to hell?

Ezekiel overheard God state the matter to his angels, as follows:—

"And to the others he said in mine hearing, Go ye after him through the city, and smite: let not your eye spare, neither have ye pity: slay utterly old and young, both maids, and little children, and women: but come not near any man upon whom is the mark; and begin at my sanctuary. Then they began at the ancient men which were before the house." (Ezek. ix. 5, 6.)

I must not at present say more on this subject; it will come more appropriately in another place.

It can not be expected that I can here note every point in Evangelicalism with which I would differ, nor go into a formal and very definite reply to any one point, for that the reader is referred to preceding portions of this volume. My chief design now is to allow Evangelicalism to speak for itself.

The first chapter of the Confession of Faith is devoted to an argument on the infallibility and perfection of the Scriptures. The second chapter to a description of the God, or rather the Gods of Evangelicalism. He is represented as being "without passions," and yet "hating sin," and will "by no means clear the guilty."

The following are the ingredients of which this God is compounded:—

In the unity of the Godhead there be *three persons*, of one substance, power, and *eternity*,—God the Father, God the Son, and God the Holy Ghost. The Father is of none, neither begotten nor proceeding; the Son is eternally begotten of the Father; the Holy Ghost eternally proceeding from the Father and the Son.—*Confession of Faith*, chap. ii. sect. 3.

This looks a little like a plurality of Gods. Here is,

"1. God the Father;

2. God the Son; and,

3. God the Holy Ghost."

These three imaginary beings are Gods, or they are not. If they are Gods, then there are *three* Gods and not one. If they are not Gods, then the above titles are wrong. Again: if they are not Gods, when taken separately, what are they? If they are men, then three men make one God. Do the followers of this creed believe that? Of course they do not! Then, are they three angels? If so, three angels will make one God; and, to find the number of Gods, all that is to be done is to group angels into bunches of three! Of course orthodoxy will not accept this.

Is God Infinite and Almighty? The Confession of Faith and Catechisms say so. Very well, then; there are in God, the Father, God the Son, and God the Holy Ghost, — three omnipotent Gods. Is not that rather more than is necessary? Does the reader say there is but one Infinite God? Then it takes three finites to make one infinite; or, these three Gods are not " of one substance, power, and eternity." Would God the Father be God without the aid of the Son or Holy Ghost? If so, these other two partners in the God-firm are only honorary and unnecessary members. If not, we fall back to the position that three *somethings* make one Infinite God. Turn this matter as you may, the absurdity of this vital point of orthodoxy can not be avoided.

Once more. What is the meaning of "eternally begotten"? Does it mean eternally in the process of being begotten? If so, he is not yet begotten. Or does it mean he is begotten for all the remainder of eternity? If so, he is, in that respect, only equal to all of us, who are eternally begotten in every sense that Jesus was.

The next chapter of this book is entitled, "Of God's Eternal Decrees." That is a contradiction of terms. A decree is an *edict* or *law*, and can not go forth without there being a time when it goes forth; but if there is a time when it is issued, there is a time *before* which it is issued; but if there is a time before which it is issued, it can not be *eternal*. So there can be no "Eternal Decrees."

The first sentence of this chapter is as follows: "God from all eternity did by the most wise and holy counsel of his own will, freely and unchangeably ordain whatsoever comes to pass."

The above being true, things are generally and specifically fixed. God did not only, "from all eternity," ordain that orthodoxy should publish an almost senseless Confession of Faith, but "did, by the most wise and holy counsel of his own will, freely and unchangeably ordain" that I should expose its nonsense. I am no more to be blamed or praised for this *exposé* than is the pen in my hand. The pen writes because I compel it to do so, and I publish this book because it was decreed from all eternity.

How strangely inconsistent this thought seems to be with the idea of prayer. Why should the believers of this doctrine pray? There is no reason in the world for it, unless it is because it was *decreed* that Christians should pray. They certainly can not expect God to answer their prayers, as it could not be done without changing an *eternal decree!* If God has decreed to do the thing Christians ask him to do, he will do them to save his decrees, not because Christians ask him. If he has not thus decreed, he has decreed the contrary, and could not be induced to violate his decree. Some of the results of this doctrine of decrees will be found in sections iii., iv., and v. of this chapter. Here they are: "By the decree of God, for the manifestation of his glory, some men and angels are predestinated unto everlasting life, and others foreordained to everlasting death."

These angels and men thus predestinated and foreordained, are particularly and unchangeably designed; and their number is so certain and definite that it can not be either increased or diminished. Those of mankind who are predestinated unto life, God, before the foundation of the world was laid, according to his eternal and immutable purpose, and the secret counsel and good pleasure of his will, he hath chosen in Christ unto everlasting glory, out of his mere free grace and love, without any foresight of faith or good works, or perseverance in either of them, or any other thing in the creature, as conditions, or causes moving him thereunto; and all to the praise of his glorious grace.

What a grand promoter of morality this must be! Your destiny is not made by your acts, but your acts and their consequences are predestinated! "The number predestinated to everlasting life is so definite, that it can not be either increased or diminished." Reader, you have nothing to do, you could not do anything if you would, and if you could it would not have any effect, otherwise it might add to or diminish from your happiness here and hereafter. As God selected you to happiness or misery, without any foresight of faith or good works on your part, your salvation or damnation is all in the hands of an arbitrary tyrant. Your good deeds can not do you or any one else any good. If you are saved at all, it is through pure, unmerited grace. Section vii. says, " The rest of mankind, God was pleased, according to the unsearchable counsel of his own will, whereby he extendeth or withholdeth mercy as he pleaseth, for the glory of his sovereign power over his creatures, to pass by, and to ordain them to dishonor and wrath for their sin, to the praise of his glorious justice."

This, with Presbyterians, may be "glorious justice;" with people who exercise more of the kind of sense called *common*, and not so much of the *dogmatical* kind, usually *dubbed theological*, it is the most damnable injustice. No demon incarnate could more thoroughly outrage every element of justice. A sovereign power that ordains "vessels of wrath," and then eternally damns them for being just what he made them, is, to say the least, fiendish. No wonder this book should urge upon its adherents to handle this doctrine of predestination "with especial prudence and care."

Chapter iv. gives the history of the Gods, whom it calls God the Father, God the Son, and God the Holy Ghost, making the world, and all there is therein, out of nothing in six literal days, The revelations of geology have caused many Christians to be careful about stepping on this rotten plank in their platform. I will only quote a single sentence. "It pleased God the Father, Son, and Holy Ghost, for the manifestation of the glory of his eternal power, wisdom, and goodness, in the beginning, to create or make of nothing the world, and all things therein, whether visible or invisible, in the space of six days, and all very good."

I now pass to chapter vi., devoted to the subject of the fall of man. I quote sections i.–iv.: "Our first parents, being seduced by the subtilty and temptation of Satan, sinned in eating the forbidden fruit. This their sin God was pleased, according to his wise and holy counsel, to permit, having purposed to order it to his own glory."

By this sin they fell from their original righteousness and communion with God, and so became dead in sin, and wholly defiled in all the faculties and parts of soul and body.

They being the root of all mankind, the guilt of this sin was imputed, and the same death in sin and corrupted nature conveyed to all their posterity descending from them by ordinary generation.

From original corruption, whereby we are utterly indisposed, disabled, and made opposite to all good, and wholly inclined to all evil, do proceed all actual transgressions.

As this has been sufficiently noticed in the first chapter of this book, but little comment is here needed.

1. We learn that the Serpent, who tempted the woman in the garden, was a no less important personage than his Satanic majesty.

2. This sin was permitted because it was for the glory of God. It does not appear from this paragraph how God was glorified, unless it is in his skill in sending the devil in the shape of a snake to tempt man and woman, and then in his ability to pronounce an unjust judgment on those who were compelled by his almighty power to act their part of the farce.

3. Although it does not appear that they had ever done a righteous act, yet by this sin they fell from original righteousness, and became *dead in sin*. That is, totally depraved. They are "wholly defiled in all their faculties and parts of the soul and body."

4. The guilt of the Adamic transgression was *imputed*. Thus we are all actually partakers of this original sin, as really as though we, in person, had stood in Adam's place.

5. We are made opposite to all good. This, I presume, is for the glory of God. Are we to blame for being made opposite to all good? What a God that must be who is glorified by making such totally depraved creatures! Reader, is Evangelicalism, thus far, a system of religion that you can believe, love, and reverence? I think not.

Section vi. of this chapter, says, "Every sin, both original and actual, being a transgression of the righteous law of God, and contrary thereunto, doth in its own nature bring guilt upon the sinner, whereby he is bound over to the wrath of God, and curse of the law, and so made subject to death, with all miseries, spiritual, temporal, and *eternal*."

Is this true? Then what becomes of a former part of this harmonious creed? If man's actual sins bring guilt upon the sinner, binding him over to the wrath of God, and rendering him subject to death, with all miseries, spiritual, temporal, and eternal, won't these actions of men spoil some of God's eternal decrees? Suppose one predestinated to eternal life happens to sin, will God save his decree by saving the man, or save this section of the Confession of Faith, and spoil his decree by damning him? If a man is damned at all, will it be because of the decree, or because of his actions?

A want of space forbids an examination of every chapter and section of the platform of Evangelical Christianity.

Section ii. of chapter viii. is so universally believed by Arminian as well as Calvinistic Christians, that I must make room for it.

"The Son of God, the second person in the Trinity,

being very and eternal God, of one substance, and equal with the Father, did, when the fullness of time was come, take upon him man's nature, with all the essential properties and common infirmities thereof, yet without sin: being conceived by the power of the Holy Ghost, in the womb of the Virgin Mary, of his substance. So that two whole, perfect, and distinct natures were inseparably joined together in one person, without conversion, composition, or confusion. Which person is very God and very man, yet one Christ, the only mediator between God and man."

Here we have a fine list of absurdities.

1. The Son of God is the very and eternal God. How can a Son be eternal? The word Son implies a Father, and the term Father implies priority of existence. But what can exist before this very and eternal God?

2. This very and eternal God is his own Son.

3. This very and eternal God is his own Father.

4. This very and eternal God is equal with his Father.

5. This very and eternal God was conceived by the power of the Holy Ghost in the womb of the Virgin Mary.

6. Wasn't that a rather naughty Ghost?

7. Would such a Ghost now be called holy?

8. If the very and eternal God was conceived in the womb of the Virgin Mary, why is not Mary the mother of God?

9. What evidence is there, beside Mary's story and Joseph's dream, that Jesus was begotten by a Ghost?

10. Would you believe a girl now who would undertake to cover her shame with such a story?

11. If her lover believed the story, even though he may have dreamed that it was true, would you not put him down as a little demented?

12. If the Godhead and Manhood in Jesus were *inseparably joined* together in the womb of the Virgin, were they *separated* in death?

13. If not, then did God die?

14. If God died, then was the world three days without a God?

15. If God did not die, then we have only a human sacrifice. What a pyramid of absurdities can be crowded into one paragraph when dictated as an explanation of Evangelicalism! How grateful am I to my risen friends that I have not been left to these delusions.

Paragraph v., of the same chapter, says, "The Lord Jesus Christ, by his perfect obedience and sacrifice of himself, which he, through the eternal spirit, once offered up unto God, hath fully satisfied the justice of his Father, and purchased not only reconciliation, but an everlasting inheritance in the kingdom of heaven, for all those whom the Father hath given unto him."

Here Jesus, the very and eternal God, offers himself as a sacrifice to the very and eternal God, — sacrifice himself to himself. Is not that a little selfish? This "has fully satisfied the justice of his Father." What a strange kind of justice that must be which decrees man to sin, and then slays his own innocent Son, the only one who is absolutely without sin, for the guilt of the world? God had decreed that man should sin; it is but just that the sufferings should be confined among the Gods; and as man only sinned because God decreed it, it is but just that man, through the suffering of God, should escape. On the ground that God is to blame for man's sins, an atonement by a God suffering is just! In this he is only partly undoing the great wrong he did in Eden, by sending a snake to tempt the woman, and ruin humanity.

Chapter ix. is devoted to the subject of *Free Will*. Section iii. says, " Man, by his fall into a state of sin, hath wholly lost all ability of will to any spiritual good accompanying salvation. So as a natural man, being altogether averse from that which is good, and dead in sin, is not able by his own strength to convert himself, or to prepare himself thereunto."

This is but another statement of the Total Depravity doctrine. " Man has *wholly* lost all ability of will to any spiritual good," and "dead in sin," &c. This being true, where is the use of exhortations? What means Peter's language, "Repent ye, therefore, and be converted." (Acts iii. 19.)

As man has no will of his own, all exhortations should be addressed to God; but as "he is unchangeable, and works all things after the counsel of his own will, and has foreordained all things, whatsoever cometh to pass," all exhortations and intercessions to him are lost! However, people will intercede if it is foreordained that they should, and my pleading is in vain. I have only one consolation: it was foreordained that I should make this plea!

"All those whom God hath predestinated unto life, and those only, he is pleased, in his appointed and accepted time, effectually to call." (Ch. x., sec. 1.)

Comments on this are unnecessary.

Section iii. says, "Elect infants, dying in infancy,

are regenerated and saved by Christ through the Spirit, who worketh when, and where, and how he pleaseth. So also are all other elect persons, who are incapable of being outwardly called by the ministry of the word."

What means the expression, "elect infants"? If it does not imply that there are infants who are not elect, there is no meaning in language. The next section fixes this matter beyond a peradventure. It is as follows: —

"Others, not elected, although they may be called by the ministry of the word, and may have some common operations of the Spirit, yet they never truly come to Christ, and therefore can not be saved: much less can men, not professing the Christian religion, be saved in any other way whatsoever, be they never so diligent to form their lives according to the light of nature, and the law of that religion they do profess; and to assert and maintain that they may, is very pernicious, and to be detested."

Those not elected, and not having gospel privileges, no matter who they are, no matter how obedient they may be to the word, "cannot be saved." See how one fatal sentence consigns over *eight hundred millions* of the present generation, who never heard of Christ, to the flames of an endless hell! "Much less can men, not professing the Christian religion, be saved in any other way whatsoever. To maintain that they are, is pernicious, and to be detested." Even admitting the truth of this beautiful (?) paragraph, why should Presbyterians be exhorted to *detest* this doctrine and its advocates? Surely it can do the elect no harm, and as for the non-elected, why not let them enjoy this as well as any other delusion? Hell is their doom at any rate, and no false doctrine can render them more miserable in the hereafter.

Chapter xi. is entitled, "Of Justification." I confess to a strong desire to reproduce the whole chapter, but can not afford the space. The first section is as follows: —

"Those whom God effectually calleth, he also freely justifieth; not by infusing righteousness into them, but by pardoning their sins, and by accounting and accepting their persons as righteous: not for any thing wrought in them, but for Christ's sake alone: not by imputing faith itself, the act of believing, or any other evangelical obedience to them, as their righteousness; but by imputing the obedience and satisfaction of Christ unto them, they receiving and resting on him and his righteousness by faith; which faith they have not of themselves: it is the gift of God."

Here the doctrine of Justification, pardon of sin or atonement, is so clearly stated, that there can be no misunderstanding it. Notice how perfectly any "righteousness of the person, or any thing wrought in them, or done by them," is ignored. It is for Christ's sake alone, "by imputing the obedience and satisfaction of Christ," "resting on him and his righteousness." Thus, Christ does it all; the sinner can do nothing. Indeed, no act of man can affect his condition in the other world. Yet these very people are afraid of Spiritualism, lest it should take away the stimulants to righteousness.

The next sentence assures us that "faith, thus receiving and resting on Christ and his righteousness, is the alone instrument of justification;" and this faith we are told, in the preceding section, is "the gift of God."

Paul says, "How can they believe on him of whom they have not heard, and how can they hear without a preacher." Where are the heathen who never heard of Christ? This theory "leaves them no refuge but hell."

The first half of the next section says, "Christ, by his obedience and death, did fully discharge the debt of all those that are thus justified, and did make a proper, real, and full satisfaction to his Father's justice in their behalf."

Now, I submit, that if "Christ has fully discharged the debt," that is all that could be justly asked. If a "proper, real, and full satisfaction" has been made in behalf of the elect, that is enough. Why should the penalty of sin, or any of it, be visited on those for whom the debt has been fully discharged, and "full satisfaction rendered to the Father." Does the reader realize what this penalty is that has been fully taken off from the elect, unless God is an unjust tyrant, dunning poor sinners for, and compelling them to pay a second time, a debt that has been fully satisfied? This Confession of Faith has said it is: "Death with all miseries, spiritual, temporal, and eternal."

The Larger Catechism says, —

2. "*What are the punishments of sin in this world?*"

Answer. The punishments of sin in this world are either inward, — as blindness of mind, a reprobate sense, strong delusions, hardness of heart, horror of conscience, and vile affections; or outward, as the curse of God upon the creatures for our sake, and all other evils that befall us in our bodies, names, estates, relations, and employments, together with death itself." (Question 28.)

In answer to Question 19, the Shorter Catechism says, "All mankind, by their fall, lost communion with God, are under his wrath and curse, and so made liable to the miseries in this life, to death itself, and the pains of hell forever." Thus we find, by all three of these standard works, that death — literal death — is the penalty of sin. Now, if "Christ has rendered full satisfaction to his Father's justice in behalf of the elect," why are they compelled to pay that part of the penalty? As no one escapes death, I must decide that there are no elect, or Evangelicalism is wrong. In either instance, would it not be well for Christians to re-examine the ground of their religion?

Section v. of the chapter under examination informs us of the impossibility of falling from grace. I wonder if the fact of so many leaving the church and coming to Spiritualism does not render some of the "elect" a little shaky on the point.

I must now pass several chapters without notice.

Chapter xvi. is a dissertation on good works. Section xii. says, "Works done by unregenerate men, although for the matter of them they may be things which God commands, and of good use both to themselves and others, yet because they proceed from a heart not purified by faith, nor are done in a right manner according to the word, nor to a right end, the glory of God, they are therefore sinful, and can not please God, or make man meet to receive grace from God." By unregenerate men, the framers of this paragraph mean *non*-Christians. What can unregenerate men, who should waste their time in reading this production conclude, but that the best they can do is to do the *worst* thing they can? Good works, which God commands, when done by them, " are sinful, and can not please God." Repentance is a good work; but, according to this, is sinful when practiced by the non-elect. Reader, according to this creed, it would be a sin for you, if you are unconverted, to haul a load of wood to keep your poor sick neighbor from freezing to death. Don't sin by taking a barrel of flour to a widow, or a pair of shoes to an orphan. This is Evangelicalism. How much will you have?

I now pass to chapter xvii.: " The Perseverance of the Saints." Sections i. and ii. certainly contain consolation for Christians. Here they are: " They whom God hath accepted in his beloved, effectually called and sanctified by his Spirit, can neither totally nor finally fall away from the state of grace, but shall certainly persevere therein to the end, and be eternally saved."

This perseverance of the saints " depends, not upon their own free will, but upon the immutability of the decree of election, flowing from the free and unchangeable love of God the Father; upon the efficacy of the merits and intercession of Jesus Christ; the abiding of the Spirit and of the seed of God within them, and the nature of the covenant of grace: from all which ariseth also the certainty and infallibility thereof."

What more could be required then? Salvation " depends, not upon their own free will, but upon the immutability of the decree of election." What can be so effectually calculated to kill all effort on the part of the people to practice the right? Enough of this. Spiritualism has helped many Christians out of such dogmas.

Reader, I have gone through this much of the Confession of Faith, not to exhibit all of its errors, but for the purpose of handing you a sample of what you are invited to take in the place of Spiritualism. An illustration of the teachings of Methodism, Campbellism, and other of the more heterodox denominations, will exhibit quite as many absurdities as are to be found in the creed just examined.

In conclusion, permit me to say Spiritualism is better than any of the Christian systems, on, at least, the following points, and for the following reasons:—

1. Because it recognizes the soul as being the only absolute authority. It fully believes every man to have an inspiration, which, if followed, will guide him as unerringly as the instinct of a bird will guide it on its wing.

2. Because it teaches that all spirit is the same, whether in God or man, and that those whom we call the *lowest* can, by virtue of their relationship with the Deity, by proper effort, develop and bring into activity the God within.

3. Because, in denying the possibility of the pardon of sin, in any sense of the word, that would permit the culprit to escape the penalty, it teaches the world to refrain from sin as the only means of happiness here and hereafter.

4. Because the evidences of its phenomena are more in harmony with reason, and better certified, than those of the Bible. Its manifestations being established by living witnesses, its evidences are better than those

of the Bible. "A living dog is better than a dead lion."

5. Because it is the only religion that teaches the absolute equality of men. Even the supposed Author of Christianity calls the Gentiles "dogs," and urges that it is not meet to take the children's bread and give it to the dogs." When he commissioned his disciples to preach, his first commission was, "Into any city of the Gentiles enter ye not." The second would not allow them to turn to the Gentiles until after the Jews had rejected the gospel. "Begin at Jerusalem," was the command.

6. Because it teaches that perfection never having been obtained by any one in this life, there is room to live a better life than ever has been, and urges upon each to take as an example the good of all historic characters, and in themselves develop some good never yet illustrated in humanity.

7. Because it is the only religion that teaches that the standard by which every one is to be judged, can not be swerved by any extraneous power, such as prayers, baptisms, sacrifices, or the blood of atonement.

8. Because, instead of looking to a future day of judgment, when an arbitrary tyrant shall reward or punish men for the belief or disbelief of a dogma, it teaches that every one shall, here and hereafter, receive the consequence of every act.

9. Because it teaches that every man must be true to his condition. It would, therefore, treat the murderer or kleptomaniac as diseased, and find a refuge and proper medical treatment for him, thus *curing* him of sin, and elevating him beyond the possibility of crime.

10. Because it makes the practice of the virtues the only path to happiness here and hereafter. It allows no supererogative works, such as prayers, confessions, and sacraments, to step between man and his duty.

11. Because it places all men on the same basis, teaching that all are members of the same family; and believing that the ultimate destiny of all is to happiness, it, instead of saying, "Let him that is filthy be filthy still," works for the reformation of those whom others recognize as incorrigible.

12. Because it teaches the principle of the fellowship of the entire human family, while Christianity only teaches the fellowship of a certain class; it urges that some "are of their father the devil," that others, on certain conditions, may become the children of our Father in heaven.

13. Because it is the only religion that teaches man that the only method of elevating himself is by the elevation of others; thus giving him a stimulus to work for others in order to help himself.

14. Because its revelations and documents are always written in the language of those for whom they are written, thus saving its adherents the valuable time and money thrown away by others in the study of languages that no amount of erudition can enable one to perfectly understand, thus giving its adherents more time for the pursuit of ethical and scientific studies.

15. Because it teaches, as did ancient heathenism, as Paul was compelled to acknowledge, that man is the offspring of God, a part and parcel of Nature, and thus invites its adherents to a study of Nature, in

order that they may understand themselves. Thus time thrown away by the representatives of other religions, in the study of a book which teaches that God and Nature are at war with each other, is, by the Spiritualists, spent in looking through science to Nature's God.

16. Because it advocates the principle of self-abnegation here, in order to happiness here and hereafter; thus enabling its adherents to endure the scoffs and sneers of an infidel Christianity.

17. Because it lifts its adherents out of a cold church materialism, and gives them a knowledge of endless life.

18. Because it calls the mind away from the weak, revengeful, passionate, illiterate human spirit the Bible calls God, and bids its adherents behold God in all Nature.

19. Because it does not compel its adherents, by forms, ceremonies, and memorials, to remember that Christ was once on earth, but bids them now find him in the persons of the afflicted, sick, imprisoned, and impoverished, and administer to his wants.

20. Because it to-day carries with it living tests that no other religion has; that the ministers of other religions dare not even see, lest they should be converted and healed.

Reader, I am now done. You have in this volume a chance to compare Evangelicalism and Spiritualism. If I have offered a thought that will benefit you, I am made happier. Heaven help us to be humble and teachable.

www.ingramcontent.com/pod-product-compliance
Lightning Source LLC
Chambersburg PA
CBHW021809230426
43669CB00008B/687